THIS PAGE IS FOR YOU!

The one major, memorable action item I
learned from reading this book is:

_____

_____

_____

_____

_____

(Don't worry, as you read the book, you'll discover
WHAT to write…and WHY!)

THEY CAN'T EAT YOU

THEY

MY UNORTHODOX PATH

CAN'T

TO OUTRAGEOUS SUCCESS

EAT

MARC SPARKS

YOU

FOREWORD BY DARREN HARDY
Publisher & Founding Editor of *SUCCESS Magazine*

PEAK

This publication is designed to provide general information regarding the subject matter covered. However, laws and practices often vary from state to state and are subject to change. Because each factual situation is different, specific advice should be tailored to the particular circumstances. For this reason, the reader is advised to consult with his or her own advisor regarding his or her specific situation.

The author and publisher have taken reasonable precautions in the preparation of this book and believe the facts presented in the book are accurate as of the date it was written. However, neither the author nor the publisher assumes any responsibility for any errors or omissions. The author and publisher specifically disclaim any liability resulting from the use or application of the information contained in this book, and the information is not intended to serve as legal, financial, or other professional advice related to individual situations.

Published by Peak Publishing, Dallas, Texas

Composition by Accelerate Media Partners, LLC, Reed Bilbray, President, Asheville, North Carolina

Dust Jacket design: Megan Sullivan

ISBN-13: 978-0-9904950-0-0

LCCN: 2014945278

Printed in the United States of America.

10 9 8 7 6 5 4 3 2 1

To my Heavenly Father Jesus Christ (Luke 12:48),
my wife Jane, my daughter Lauren, my mom Jo McIntyre,
my dad Jim Sparks, and my friends and colleagues—
Trish Rodgers, Megan Sullivan, Chris Kraft, Mark Hitchner,
Greg Schardt, Jimmy Sparks (my brother), Jeff Johnson,
George Thompson, Lynne Sipiora, Laura Morton, Dan Dunn,
Darren Hardy, Paul Slack, and all of the "A-Teamers"—
thank you all for making such profound
contributions in my life.

The Samaritan Inn is a Dallas-area homeless shelter that provides a hand up, not a handout. Our current facility houses 160 residents, one-third of which are children, each night. We are always 100 percent occupied, and we are forced to turn away 50 to 75 people a week due to overcapacity challenges. The Samaritan Inn Village, anticipated to be under construction at the end of 2014, will house over 500 people!

www.TheSamaritanInn.org

Contents

Foreword

by Darren Hardy, Publisher and Founding Editor, *SUCCESS* Magazine

We have more diet books than ever, yet as a species we are fatter than ever. We have more books than ever about building a business, yet more businesses are failing. Why is this? It's because most books lie to you, and most authors are full of hooey. (Note: the editor made me change my original word). Most books are written by people who have never done themselves (in an extraordinary manner) what they are telling you to do, and they pontificate about some new shortcut or magic formula for how to succeed. Most spend more time positioning themselves as experts than they do offering expertise. Here's the deal: there are no shortcuts. The game isn't fair. Business is a bare-knuckle brawl, and to become a champion, you're gonna get your nose bloodied along the way. People don't like to hear that for some reason, but it's the truth. Thomas Edison said it long ago: "Opportunity is missed by most people because it's dressed in overalls and looks like work."

Marc Sparks has done it. BIG. Over and over again (and continues to). And this book tells you the truth about succeeding in business.

I've been waiting for this book for nearly a decade. Before building SUCCESS Media and becoming publisher and founding editor of *SUCCESS* magazine, I was president of The Success Training Network (TSTN), owned by Marc. I saw firsthand the street-smart, profoundly wise, and intuitive genius that was Marc Sparks. But most of his magic was still an enigma to me. I wanted the mystery solved. I wanted to learn how he did it—all of it—plainly and completely.

But Marc is incredibly illusive. The truth is, he is either shy, private, humble, or all the above. It takes all the verbal judo I have to get him to talk about himself even for a minute or two! I pushed him for years to write this book . . . and I'm not the only one pushing. Almost everyone who has worked for him, with him, or against has pushed him to write this book. A group of his leaders even staged a coup while visiting him at his home in Aspen, Colorado. They called it the Colorado Intervention.

At the end of a five-day dude trip filled with golf and fly-fishing, the timing seemed right. Toward the bottom of a great bottle of wine (persuasion always goes better at the end of a bottle), while sitting together on his back veranda overlooking an expansive valley and the sunset-lit Rocky Mountains strung out all along the horizon, they pounced . . . and the intervention commenced. Every member of the small circle took turns with his best pitch—passionately trying to convince Marc to write the very book you are about to read.

Marc was caught off-guard, and once he figured out what was really going on, he winced, squirmed, flicked his hand in disregard, and tried to laugh it off. Even after several attempts to change the subject and redirect the conversation—something Marc is normally quite skilled at doing—the group wouldn't back down. Trouble is, Marc had none of the typical hot buttons for why people write books: self-adulation, promotion, fame. Even the thought of it all made him cringe.

Then they finally hit pay dirt. Marc's cofounder of Splash Media, Chris Kraft, said, "Marc, what if you just help one entrepreneur and it makes all the difference in his or her business? Think about it: if you don't write this book, that one person might not make it."

Then Marc's favorite Bible verse was brought into the conversation to land the knockout punch: "For everyone to whom much is given, of him shall much be required; and from the one to whom much has been entrusted, even more will be demanded" (Luke 12:48). When Marc asked my opinion, I sided with Luke.

I asked, "Marc, how many people have helped you succeed?"

"Many," was his response.

"Then it's time to pay it forward," I said. "It's a responsibility. You have an obligation to write this book." I was pushing Marc because I truly felt his hard-fought nuggets of wisdom packaged up in a book could make a profound impact on the business future of many entrepreneurs. And, quite frankly, I wanted a better look behind the curtain of Oz myself.

Marc is the epitome of a self-made success story. He never went to college, didn't inherit any seed money, and did not come from notable DNA. Marc started with nothing and built empire after empire from the construct of his mind and the grit of his determination. Marc has that rare, anything-is-possible, no-fear, fail-fast drive. He believes that the sooner you fail, the sooner you will succeed—a model that has proven to work for him repeatedly.

While Marc is not as publicly known as many of the über achievers you've seen on the cover of *SUCCESS*, he shares many of their attributes. He has the "Screw it, let's do it! If you fall flat on your face, get up and try again" mindset of Richard Branson. Like

Branson, Marc doesn't hear "No," he only hears "Try harder." Fear and failure don't frighten or paralyze him; rather, they intrigue and invigorate him.

Marc has the same "Sure we can inhabit Mars" audacious courage and wild ambition of an Elon Musk. When others think he's crazy, he is willing to make the big bet using his own wallet to fuel the rocket ship of his wild ideas. Marc sees the world in terms of what's possible and how fast (dubbed "Sparks Speed") through the same reality distortion field Steve Jobs did. Marc and Steve also share the same standard of quality and excellence, and have an intuitive sense for beautiful design and the genius of great packaging.

Like Jeff Bezos (Amazon) and Howard Schultz (Starbucks), Marc has a keen ability to find the magic factor that will ignite an enterprise and make it scale. Then he has the relentless discipline to keep everything else simple and focused on the fundamentals, just as John Wooden does.

Marc has the humble and affable quality, mixed with the negotiation prowess of Warren Buffett. They both have been known to make a multimillion-dollar deal on the back of an envelope, secured by a handshake. And in the end, they will own the heart of the deal and still leave you feeling victorious.

And maybe most importantly Marc has a sincere caring for people, similar to Tony Hsieh (Zappos) or Joel Osteen. He treats people right, fairly, and generously. He is well respected and trusted because he gives both respect and trust first.

What makes Marc different and exceptional in my eyes is that he is the rare man who has the combination of all those attributes. We can all learn a great deal from a man like Marc.

The way I see it is, this book gives you the privilege to learn from the man in the arena:

"The credit belongs to the man who is actually in the arena, whose face is marred by dust and sweat and blood; who strives valiantly; who errs, who comes short again and again, because there is no effort without error and shortcoming; but who does actually strive to do the deeds; who knows great enthusiasms, the great devotions; who spends himself in a worthy cause; who at the best knows in the end the triumph of high achievement, and who at the worst, if he fails, at least fails while daring greatly, so that his place shall never be with those cold and timid souls who neither know victory nor defeat."

—Theodore Roosevelt, 1910

You can save lots of your own sweat and blood by studying the pages ahead. Certainly your face will still become marred in dust as you enthusiastically strive to pursue your own worthy cause, but at least you can gain direct tutelage from one who himself has dared greatly, fought valiantly, and claimed repeated victories. The man in the ring has chronicled his unorthodox methods so you too can experience the triumph of high achievement and outrageous success in the ring of business and life. Enjoy!

Darren Hardy
Summer 2014

Preface

I've never been the kind of guy who likes to talk about myself, so the thought of writing a book, while daunting, wasn't nearly as scary as the idea of writing a book about my least favorite topic—me. Throughout my career, colleagues have often suggested that I take time to record my thoughts about business and life. These are all people with whom I've done business for years, even decades. They all know me well; they each know bits and pieces of my history, but none of them have all of the pieces of the puzzle.

During a 2011 fly-fishing trip to Colorado, I was ambushed by three close colleagues and friends. Chris Kraft and Paul Slack, cofounders of Splash Media Agency, and Mark Hitchner, CEO of Splash Media University, wanted me to bite the bullet and pen a book. I listened as each spoke to me about why I had to do it.

Chris started by telling me, "Working with you has been an education I will take with me for the rest of my career. Your style isn't standard start-up stuff. It's more 'real-world MBA.' You've always told me anyone can have a great idea, but success or failure depends on the execution and on whether you believe in your ability to shape the vision. I'm the kind of guy who can see a business in the future, but you see it in 3-D. You don't see the bricks—you see the house. You've got too much good information in your head to not share it."

Mark continued with this: "You're not an 'it has to be perfect' kind of guy. You're more interested in building something of value to others, something that is made well and done with excellence. You've always told me that you are a builder. Even though I have my MBA, 80 percent of what I have learned about business has come from working with you. Aren't you the guy who always tells me, 'If you don't go out there and put forth the effort and try, you won't get anywhere'?"

And just in case I wasn't convinced, Paul added, "Even though I haven't been in the family as long as Chris and Mark have, one thing I quickly learned is that your pace is a speed at which you don't spend a lot of time thinking through every last detail. You just go, go, and do. I used to try to build my future by creating flowcharts and guessing at what might happen. You go out and create a future based on your vision. You shape the outcome instead of allowing it to shape you. You are one of the most brilliant men with whom I've ever worked, especially when it comes to seeing opportunity and not being afraid to fail. You are also the most comfortable human being I have ever met. You know who you are and what you're all about. How many people can really make that same claim? That, in and of itself, is a secret worth sharing."

So there it was. The guys laid out their case for me, and I had to admit they had a point. Their insistence gave me a lot to think about. I know most people read these types of books for inspiration, but I wasn't sure how many of them would actually get up and make the changes that I would suggest. I believe that most people want to change but lack the discipline to follow through. If I were to make the commitment to share my views widely, my goal would be to get you, the reader, to follow my message. I wasn't sure it would be possible, but uncertainty has never been a deterrent in my life or my businesses. In fact, I get excited by the challenge of what others see as impossible. After all, I am a living example of someone who never should have made it, but did.

While I consider myself to be the quintessential serial entrepreneur, I am what many would perceive as the anti-business businessman. Most of my methods are the opposite of what you think you already know, of what you've learned in business school, and most certainly of current mainstream business practices. I believe business plans are for village idiots, titles are for people with no confidence, and that the smartest guy in the room isn't necessarily the one who will succeed.

One of my strongest beliefs in business and everyday life comes from a verse in the Bible: "For everyone to whom much is given, of him shall much be required; and from the one to whom much has been entrusted, even more will be demanded" (Luke 12:48).

You don't get a free pass in life. When you receive, you must give back. Over the course of the past thirty years, I have spent a great deal of time and resources giving back, including my work with The Samaritan Inn, the America Can! Academy, Sparky's Kids, and others. I'm certainly not perfect, but I sure want to give back as much as I can, and I'm doing it as fast as I can before I die.

At fifty-six years young, I have also grown extremely confident and comfortable in my own skin, enough so that I have come to realize that the nuggets of wisdom I have gathered over the years might actually mean something to other people who are trying to carve their own pathways to success. People come to me all the time with good ideas but no clue how to get them off the ground. MBA or not, they are totally lost. Maybe my true calling—my purpose—is to give entrepreneurs nuggets (I call them "Sparks") of wisdom and the tools that will help set them on the right course. And since I can't meet with every entrepreneur who has a business idea, I'd like to share some of my insights with you here, in this book.

Was This Book Written for You?

This book was written for a very special person. Not a single person, mind you, but a person who fits a certain profile. It's very possible that you fit the profile I had in mind when I first set out on this journey.

- If you look at life a bit differently than those around you do, this book was written for you.

- If you see opportunity everywhere, this book was written for you.

- If you know deep down inside that you have more to give this world than just the time between punching a clock, this book was written for you.

- If you question the status quo and so-called experts, this book was written for you.

- If you have a desire to make an impact on the world and not just on your own life, this book was written for you.

- If you are open to new ways of thinking and are willing to toss out much of what you learned in school, this book was written for you.

- If you are striving for success but finding it elusive, this book was written for you.

- If you want to live a more fulfilling life, this book was definitely written for you.

This may sound pretentious, but I have unlocked the secrets to being successful—not just in business, but also in life. Sure sounds bold and full of puffery, doesn't it? Even so, I sincerely believe it's true. If I didn't, I promise I would not have wasted your time or mine writing this book.

You will get nothing out of this book if you just read the words. You have to take action and apply what you learn. Life is full of talkers, dreamers, and wannabes. Maybe you have lived your life in one of those categories in the past, and there is absolutely nothing wrong with that. However, I suspect that you want more out of life and the world around you, and that's why you found this book . . . or why it found you.

Do not waste the opportunity you have at this moment. Don't just reach for your goals; make up your mind right now that you will achieve those goals. Push yourself to answer whatever calling you may have. It is my hope that this book will provide you with solid action items that will help you attain what you want and be outrageously successful in anything you do.

My hope is that you will mine one or two valuable nuggets from the ideas and stories that led me down my unorthodox path to success. If by chance you get more than that, my greatest goal in writing this book will have been fulfilled.

If you have an entrepreneur's heart, this book is for you!

Make This Book WORK for You!

Are you ready to get started? Are you really ready to act on what you learn from my journey to success?

If so, then there are a few things you must do before we begin. If you really want to succeed and get the very most out of this book and my many years of experience—years that have earned me the equivalent of a Ph.D. as an entrepreneur—I suggest you do the following:

- Break out a yellow highlighter and run it over every word of wisdom that inspires you.

- Get a blue ink pen (not black) and make notes to yourself in the margin; the blue will be easy to read beside the black print on the page.

- Mark this book up as if you are mad at the world!

- Read every highlight and every note you made, at 6:12 p.m. on Sundays, for the next six weeks.

- Identify one major, memorable action item you learned from reading this book, and write it on the first page of this book. Just one!

- Let me know when you have had a major milestone from reading my book. Ping me on one of my social media sites. I would love to know that my experiences have made a difference in your life.

> www.twitter.com/msparks5010
>
> www.linkedin.com/in/marcsparks
>
> www.facebook.com/marc.sparks1

Focus is the primary key to accomplishing anything. It's easy to get derailed by everyday life, so staying concentrated and committed to whatever it is you're aiming for is how you get things done. The points made in this book reflect how I get things done. They're sensible, logical, and even controversial. I'm okay with that because, as Socrates once said, "The only true wisdom is knowing you know nothing." And as Benjamin Franklin added, "A wise man does not need advice, and a fool won't take it."

Think of this book as a tool for higher learning. As with any education, building a strong knowledge base is best, even if you don't get to use the information you're storing in your head all the time. It's good to know it's there, though, especially for the budding entrepreneur who can learn from other people's experiences and avoid making the same mistakes or choices along the path.

ORTHODOX PATH: Read this book, put it on a shelf, and forget what you read a week later.

SPARKS PATH: Get a highlighter and a blue pen and mark this book up like you're mad at it. Read your markups every Sunday evening at 6:12 for six weeks.

PART ONE

Schadenfreude

You're probably reading this book because you heard about an average, high-school-educated entrepreneur who has had some outrageous successes and some colossal disasters . . . and you can't wait to read about his pain. It's okay. I realize that our society wants to make sure that the successful guy (me) has had his share of discomfort and strife. The Germans have a word for this: *schadenfreude*. Pronounced "shah-den-froi-da," it means "to enjoy the suffering of others." In the spirit of satisfying society's morbid desire to witness the suffering of others, I promise you will not be disappointed when reading this book.

In 1987, I was a 29-year-old guy who had barely squeaked by in high school. I graduated with a C+ average from Westlake High in Austin, Texas, and I was ready to conquer the world, although I had absolutely no means to do so. Despite the odds, by age 29, I—with an unbridled, entrepreneurial spirit—had already made my first couple million dollars . . . and lost it again. I didn't lose it to wild parties and overindulgence; I lost it to more ventures. However, I wasn't remotely deterred—after all, true risk is doing nothing at all. I didn't have any money, but I had received my degree in hard knocks, and I was dealt some pretty fantastic cards. I was a young, healthy, white male in the greatest, most opportunistic country in the world. I was full of confidence and drive, and I had no fear of failing. Little did I know that after my very next venture, I would be wildly successful . . . and then have to spend four years of my life and a million dollars in legal fees, just trying to stay out of prison.

Unistar

In August 1989, I started Consolidated Surety Agency, a construction surety bond company in Dallas, Texas. Over the next ten years, it became the insurance conglomerate known as Unistar. The company began modestly in my one-bedroom apartment, where we wrote construction surety payment and performance bonds for contractors all over the country on federal, state, and municipal projects. A surety bond written on a construction project guarantees the owner that the contractor will pay his bills and complete the project within a set period of time. Typically, the owner would pay between 1.5 percent and 3 percent of the project value as a premium (fee to the insurance company) for the payment and performance surety bonds. On a $10 million dollar project, the cost could be as much as $300,000 to guarantee that a contractor would perform and pay his subcontractors. Should the contractor default, the owner of the project would inform the surety company to investigate the matter, which usually resulted in the insurance company writing a lot of big checks to cover the contractor's breech.

At the time, many smaller construction companies didn't have this type of coverage because it was difficult to obtain. When

I realized how hard it was for these small companies to access surety bonding, I knew in my gut a business opportunity existed for anyone who could successfully provide this service. I quickly figured out what it would take to make bonding available to the masses, and that's how Consolidated Risk Management was born. The company performed as an escrow agent between the contractor and the project owner. All project proceeds (millions of dollars) were sent to my firm for disbursement to subcontractors and suppliers. That way, we were pretty much guaranteed that the bills would get paid. The fee for our services ranged between 2 percent and 4 percent of the value of the project, with the fees normally paid by the contractor. Without these construction risk management services, the contractor simply could not get bonding and, therefore, could not do the work. We were excited about this idea and quickly became the front runner in the industry. Although we were the first company to blaze a trail in this arena, many competitors have since flourished from the idea.

My business grew extremely fast and was ridiculously successful. Within months, I had a dozen full-time staff members working with me to help fulfill the ever-expanding needs of our clients. We couldn't write the surety bonds fast enough to keep up with the demand. As my business platform grew, the company began to take on a life of its own. My ultimate goal was to provide surety bonding and insurance for every need a person could possibly have, from cradle to grave. In a relatively short time, my business morphed into a multibillion-dollar property and casualty insurance machine. Moving at a pace my friends and colleagues fondly call Sparks Speed, I quickly acquired other insurance licenses in addition to my local recording agent's insurance license, a surplus lines license, and a managing general agent's license. I spent the next ten years of my life working toward my dream of fully integrating my insurance businesses so that all potential needs could be met under one umbrella.

My vision wasn't just selling insurance to the consumer; I wanted to service the policy, manage every claim, finance the premiums, and even share in the insurance risk. Over the years, our primary focus shifted from the construction industry to the automobile insurance industry, where we could service a policy all the way to the collision repair—because we eventually owned several auto body shops as well. Of course, insured individuals could get as many collision estimates as they wanted, and they could work with whichever body shop they chose, but more often than not, they selected our shops because our estimates were usually the most economical. Owning every part of the process meant that when our auto insurance clients came to us for repairs on their cars, it not only made the process seamless for them, but also lucrative for us. At the time, the concept was revolutionary.

Before we decided to go with the name Unistar, the parent company of the different businesses I owned was called U.S. Fidelity Holding Corp. The divisions below that banner rivaled competitors GEICO, State Farm, Progressive, and almost every other insurance provider out there. We owned nearly 200 insurance agency offices in Texas, California, and Florida, with our sights set on expansion into another ten states. We were successfully partnered with eleven A and A+ rated reinsurers from all over the world. A reinsurer is an insurer that assumes a portion of the entire insurance risk portfolio. If, for example, we wrote $100 million worth of top-line revenue, a reinsurer might take 10 percent or 20 percent of that risk based on our performance record and a litany of underwriting and background investigations they conducted on us. Bringing together such a stellar, first-class list of reinsurers to back my business remains one of the crowning achievements in my thirty-five-year entrepreneurial career. At the time, I could not have been prouder.

To receive A and A+ rated (by A.M. Best) reinsurance, as an insurance provider, our business had to be audited and dissected many times each year to make sure our company was rock solid and worthy of those reinsurers' trust. In fact, I can't remember a day when an auditor was not present in our offices. We withstood their rigorous tests every time, so much so that we were backed by $12 billion worth of reinsurers. They knew we wrote a lot of business and were good at what we were doing, so they practically gave us a blank check's worth of authority to write as much insurance as we could sell.

By 1996, as one of the final steps to fully completing my vision, we purchased a distressed property and casualty insurance company in an arrangement with the Texas Department of Insurance. Simultaneously, I applied for and received what's referred to as "Form A" approval, which is the equivalent of getting the state's blessing to own and operate a full-fledged insurance company (not just an agency). This final piece empowered us to grow Unistar into one of the most successful, privately owned insurance holding corporations in the nation. Throughout it all, we placed our focus on business development and quality customer service, which helped us grow and profit exponentially.

In 1998, at the peak of our success, Unistar employed close to 1,000 people; had nearly 200 retail agency offices in California, Texas, and Florida; and had over 600 appointed agents selling our insurance products in three of the most populated states in the country. We also owned two licensed premium finance companies, an insurance company, and several collision repair centers. We were generating over $200 million in top-line revenue.

Our home office in Dallas was located in a 30,000-square-foot warehouse building we had purchased and renovated, which was a new concept back then. We were a force to be reckoned with. At the time, I could have sold the company privately for between $150 million and $300 million.

Unistar appeared to be unstoppable. It was remarkable: I was leading a company that was making positive changes in an industry I thought of as vital to the good people we insured. I was helping my team grow their own careers and wealth while finding ways to give back to the community and those in need. It was everything I had dreamed of and more . . . but it wouldn't last.

Going Public

In spring 1998, I was trying to figure out a way for my hardworking team to reap greater benefits from the successes we were experiencing. I was approached by a group of investment bankers, brought to me via a mutual acquaintance, to see if I had an interest in taking Unistar public. After some convincing, I figured this was the perfect way for everyone—from the agents in the field to the top brass—to become true owners in our collective destiny. Going public also gave me the currency (stock) to acquire more agencies and to provide incentive to key individuals who I'd hoped would never leave me. I jumped all over this opportunity, as it seemed to be the perfect plan.

I had been considering the possibility of taking the company public for some time, so when the offer was put on the table, I believed it was divinely inspired. You see, my ultimate vision was to find a way for this incredibly hardworking, smart group of people to become shareholders of our company, making them wealthy in the process. Taking Unistar public would accomplish this virtually overnight. I always thought it made perfect sense to give my team ownership in the company where they worked so they never felt as if their work were simply a J.O.B. If everyone has a vested interest in performing at a higher level and in rowing the boat in the same direction, we would gain tremendous momentum and become virtually unstoppable. This was a move I took right out of Sam Walton's playbook, when he gave his employees ownership in Walmart. I believe it is only right that everyone shares in success. Ownership in a thriving company also acts as "golden handcuffs"—employees don't wonder what life would be like working at a competitor's business.

It didn't take long to put together the formal offering. On September 9, 1998, Unistar began trading for $26 a share. In May 1999, I found myself ringing the opening bell on Wall Street because Unistar had moved its stock listing to the American Stock Exchange and was trading at $41 a share. I could barely contain my excitement at being on the trading floor that day. I'm not much of a crying kind of a guy, but on that day, I was overcome with emotion. I wept like a baby. A decade of indescribably hard work had finally paid off. Everyone was happy. WE DID IT! We felt like we had climbed Mount Everest, swum the English Channel, and won the gold medal in the 100-meter dash at the Olympics— all in record time and all in one day. Later that night, I couldn't help but wonder—how did a kid with a C+ average in high school end up ringing the bell on Wall Street for a wildly successful, trailblazing insurance holding company? I remember eating in the formal dining room that day with the chairman of the American Stock Exchange and about ten others, and also receiving a brass desk clock with an engraving of our milestone on the back. It was an unforgettable, significant gesture. While writing this book, fifteen years after that time, I took the clock out of a box and put it on the shelf in my office. Just thinking about this profound experience still makes me well up.

As promised, everyone at Unistar was issued their shares, all of which were customarily restricted. That meant they had to hold the stock for a period of time until it vested before they were allowed to sell it. The purpose of this practice (called Rule 144) is to ensure there would not be a run on the bank the first day of trading. Those who bought the Unistar stock through general trading sources were issued common, freely tradable shares. It was one of the biggest thrills of my life. I thought my dreams had all come true and that this event would impact hundreds of people in a very positive way for the rest of their lives.

By July 1999, Unistar was trading at an all-time high of $61.63 a share and had over a $1 billion market cap. While common today, it was hard for me to believe that the value of our stock had shot up that significantly in such a short period of time—but it had. It's not as though I had my head in the sand or my fingers in my ears; I simply had no reason to suspect that catastrophe would strike.

I thought everything was going better than expected. I was running the company as solidly as I had been when we were privately held, so for me, it was business as usual—except there were a lot more people to answer to than when we were private. Investors called the office daily, wanting to know how things were going. They asked all types of questions, which we always did our best to answer. We frequently sent out press releases with performance reports and news of exciting acquisitions and milestones. We kept the public relations moving in a forward direction so everyone had the same information as we did. Operationally, Unistar was outrageously successful, and the sky was the limit. But, unbeknownst to me, everything in my world was about to come crashing down.

Doomsday 1999

Doomsday began on July 17, 1999. The stock of the company (not the company itself) was brutally attacked by short sellers. Short sellers prey on public companies whose stock prices seem to rise too fast. Unnaturally, a short seller wants the stock price to go down and, in fact, is betting that the stock's price will go down. In many cases, they actually create false negative rumors so the stock becomes questionable (a practice even more common today with the advent of the Internet). These rumors often incite a fear-based sell-off, causing the stock value to fall like a lead balloon. Today, several short-selling laws in place might have prevented our catastrophic demise; however, dwelling on the fact that these laws didn't exist then would be like crying over spilled milk. We were not prepared for such an attack, and the chaos that followed simply took control.

From July 13–16, 1999, Unistar's stock inexplicably fell from around $62 a share with nearly a billion-dollar market cap to its lowest price of $27 a share. It was a 55 percent decline over the course of three days. On July 23, the U.S. Securities and Exchange Commission (SEC) actually suspended trading of the stock, pending a review of the sharp and sudden drop in price. Their informal investigation was standard procedure for a trading halt on a relatively new listing, but it didn't make me feel any better for our staff and our shareholders. Somewhere, someone was shorting our stock in a malicious attempt to destroy our company. The short sellers were making millions of dollars in the process, while a lot of unsuspecting and hardworking people (including me) had been financially devastated and left in a path of destruction with the worst of the storm yet to come. Interestingly enough, we never found out who was behind the decimation of our stock. I always suspected it might have been one of our shrewd competitors. The Internet was just starting to gain traction, and although the means to take a negative rumor viral did not exist then as they do today, there were some tools that could be used to crush a stock electronically. Unfortunately, none were advanced enough to allow us to track who was behind it.

When the SEC halted trading, they did so in support of Unistar. They were trying to figure out what was going on and fast. And they were not alone; my board and I wanted to understand what was happening, too, as soon thereafter, I was the one ultimately accused of releasing false statements and engaging in manipulative acts to defraud our shareholders. These false allegations hit me hard, especially because they couldn't have been further from the truth. When I heard the comments people were making about me, I thought, *They must be talking about someone else.* I couldn't identify with anything they were saying.

"He cheated us!" "He lied!" "He profited while we lost . . ." And I heard much worse.

I'm not especially good with dates, but I will never forget November 5, 1999. I, along with ten members of my board of directors, received a letter via Federal Express from the SEC informing us that Unistar—and several of its key executives— was under formal investigation. My heart sank, and my mouth went bone dry. My home phone started ringing off the hook that morning at 7:30. Over the years, I had assembled an outstanding and distinguished board of directors, and we were building a remarkable insurance holding company. Several of these board members were successful attorneys and insurance professionals whom I had known for many years, and it was an honor when each of them accepted a seat on my board. You can imagine my shock and embarrassment when these colleagues were dragged into an SEC investigation. Sheer and utter shame was my first emotion, followed quickly by disbelief and dismay. The "shorts" had made a lot of money—millions on the way up—and now they had made a bloody fortune on the crash down.

In an effort to decipher what was really happening and to see how we could limit the damage, I called a board meeting as soon as possible. Before I had the chance to say a word, the board of directors asked me—their founder, chairman, and CEO—to step down. I went to that meeting believing we were all in this nightmare together; they came to the meeting intending to stage a coup. They wanted to fire me from my own company! The insurance company division president was the only person who stood up to the board members, saying, "This is insane. We are throwing out the founder, the day-to-day rainmaker of this organization." His plea fell on deaf ears. Like rats jumping from a sinking ship, it was every man for himself.

I was the single largest shareholder, and still they gave me no choice but to walk away and try to preserve some of my dignity. They were hell-bent on seeing me crumbled and destroyed. There was so much undeserved anger coming my way. I had never experienced anything quite like it, yet I stood there and took their wrath because I was the leader of our company—the leader who had made the fateful decision to take Unistar public. I easily could have sold my private company for more than $250 million, but I swung for the fences with the bases loaded. It seemed I had no choice but to take the corporate fall. The business was quite sound, but the public stock damage and the SEC's investigation created instant distrust with our $12 billion worth of A-rated reinsurers. Over time, our reinsurance was slowly dismantled. Without reinsurance, we were sunk. In this case, the billion-dollar baby clearly had been thrown out with the bath water.

SCREECH! WHAM! CRASH! An eighteen-wheeler with a full load coming out of nowhere and smashing into the side of my car . . . that's one way to describe the feeling I had when I lost Unistar. In a flash, nearly all that I loved in the world had been taken away from me. Poof! It was gone! Life, as I knew it, was over.

My personal family was intact (thank God), but I had lost my work family in that horrific accident. That is exactly how it felt to have Unistar and ten years of fourteen-hour workdays just slip through my fingers. That is precisely the image I see every time I close my eyes and think about that life-shattering experience. A lot of people lost wealth as a result of the fall of Unistar. They were good, honest people who did all the right things through the years to ensure their futures. They were people who trusted me to make sure they would someday get where they hoped and dreamed of being. When we issued stock to the majority of our staff, many of them became instant millionaires on paper. Some took what they thought was their newfound affluence and lived as if they already had the money in the bank. Others understood that they weren't wealthy quite yet, as they couldn't sell their shares until the stock was vested. They didn't change their lifestyle based on an assumed value, and they weren't wounded as deeply as those who did. Any way you look at it, all of my people expected me to guide them through the devastation—but that was something I could no longer do. My heart was shattered—not just for my losses, but for theirs as well.

After four grueling, painful years of interrogation, document discovery, depositions, legal expenses, public humiliation, and tremendous lost opportunities, I was set free with a small fine. The SEC gave me two options: pay a $50,000 fine and agree not to sit on a public board for five years, or pay a $100,000 fine and have the option to sit on any public board at any time. Both options allowed me to move forward while neither admitting nor denying any wrongdoing. In the end, I decided to take the $100,000 option, as I did not want to give anyone the satisfaction of restricting my freedom to sit on a public board. I have no desire to sit on a public board, nor do I ever plan to; however, it was worth an additional $50,000 to ensure that the option was mine and not theirs.

A decade and a half later, I still find it hard to drive past my old Unistar building. In a strange way, writing this book has helped me deal with the tragedy, and now I can actually speak about it out loud. I have accepted that this was my journey, and I have embraced it. Tough times don't last—tough people do! My wife Jane was my rock throughout the entire ordeal. She never complained, never judged. It's often said that behind every good man is a great woman, and boy, there has never been a truer statement. Although I have always done my best to leave the strain of business at the office and out of our home and marriage, this time it was unavoidable. There was no hiding the fact that I was falling apart. As it turns out, I was clinically depressed—something I never expected to experience and something I wasn't prepared to handle on my own. My doctor put me on Prozac to help get me through what he described as a temporary ailment, and I am so grateful he did. Within a few weeks, I started feeling like myself again, and I weaned myself off the medication because it made me feel as though I was losing my edge.

One of my true blessings is that I am not the kind of man who crumbles under pressure, nor do I take defeat as an ending. I see it as a challenge to win next time. I knew I would somehow pick up the pieces of my life and move forward into new and unconquered frontiers. After all, if I didn't, *they* would have won.

Jumping Back In

As soon as my few short days of self-pity were over, I sought my next venture. I had to get back in the game. The industry I had intimately known for a decade—insurance—was off the table, as no one would take my calls. It was clear that I had to move on.

Martin Luther King Jr. once said, "The ultimate measure of a man is not where he is in times of comfort, but where he stands in moments of challenge and controversy." I was determined to rebuild my life. I wasn't even sure how much money I had lost in the debacle. I might have been bankrupt, too, had I lived above my means. Thankfully, due to my disdain for debt, I had a house that was paid for and the ability to borrow against it if needed. There was no point in trying to figure out the details of what had really happened, because that would be like looking in a rearview mirror. I couldn't go back if I were ever to move forward again.

I called Trish Coulman (now Rodgers) and told her I was ready to start completely over and asked if she was ready to do it with me. I'll never forget when she said, "I was wondering when you were going to snap out of it!" For years, she had been by my side. When I stepped down from Unistar, she stepped down with me. It was very Jerry McGuire-ish of her. There was no question that Trish was loyal, and as we walked out the doors that fateful day, she had turned to me and said, "What do we do now?" At the time, I simply didn't have an answer for her, but I knew we'd eventually find something and kick butt again!

They Can't Eat You

In Africa, when a zebra has a bad day, he doesn't get to start from scratch. He gets eaten! *At least*, I told myself, *They can't eat you!* One thing I was blessed with was the gift of confidence. I am either the most ignorant guy in the world or one of the boldest, because it suddenly occurred to me that no matter how bad things got, they couldn't eat me. Even if the SEC and the Department of Justice had come up with something and thrown me in jail, I'd still be alive. I started with nothing, and I could start all over again with nothing. I wanted to *build* something again. The problem was that I didn't know what that something would be, so I decided to let others bring their ideas to me.

Mr. Gwinn

"Trish, let's place an ad in the paper," I declared as confidently as though I had just discovered penicillin. I wanted people with cool business ideas to bring them to me to see what we could do to help launch their products (my early version of *Shark Tank*). I've always been a big believer in all forms of media, so it wasn't a novel idea to place the ad, but the content of the ad itself was risky and bold. I remember reading that, in 1968, John Roberts and Joel Rosenman, the organizers of the Woodstock Music Festival, had taken out an ad that read, "Young men with unlimited capital are looking for interesting and legitimate investment opportunities and business propositions." Shortly afterward, Michael Lang and Artie Kornfeld approached them with the idea of building a recording studio in Woodstock, New York. They named their new company Woodstock Ventures, Inc. To promote their new studio to musicians, they wanted to host a music festival. And the rest, as they say, is history.

I wrote a tombstone-style ad to be placed in the business section of *The Dallas Morning News*. On the morning of December 5, 1999, there it was:

NEED CAPITAL?

Investment firm is seeking dynamic D/FW companies in need of capital. Owners must remain; companies must be at least one year old (no restaurants). Prefer e-commerce, high-tech businesses, and manufacturing. But will consider retail. Equity participating funds provides capital, management, and marketing assistance where needed. Fax outline of capital needs, business summary, and financials to

MR. GWINN AT 972-387-XXXX.

Fifteen years later, I still have that fax number and a framed copy of the ad. I specifically stated that I wasn't interested in restaurants because I had already dabbled in that arena during my twenties. It was a good business, but not the direction I wanted to go. I used a pseudonym so no one would know where they were actually sending their materials. I wasn't trying to hide; I was merely trying to shield myself from every Tom, Dick, and Harry looking for a handout.

We received somewhere around 300 responses, including several business plans that were hand-delivered to my office instead of faxed. I don't know how they found me, and I had specifically stated that I didn't want anything but a fax. My thought was simple: if you can't follow directions out of the gate, what makes you think anyone would consider financing your venture? I have always believed that business plans are completely worthless and irrelevant. Tell me about you and your product. Get my attention, and then let's figure out how we can succeed together.

Trish and I went through each of the responses and determined which ones met my criteria. A few days later, Trish came across a paragraph-long letter written by the girlfriend of a software inventor. She had written this on behalf of her boyfriend: "Give me 15 minutes of your time, and I will show you my stock-trading software tool that will change the world." Something about it got Trish's attention. It was bright and intriguing enough that she put it on my desk with a sticky note attached that read, "You should call this guy."

When George walked through the door, I could tell he was an aggressive entrepreneur. He was young, smart, working out of his living room . . . and stuck in inventor's hell. George had a great idea and product, and his timing was perfect; however, he lacked the know-how or resources to get it launched. He had sold a few hundred applications of his software through a couple of trade shows, his beta test to see how the product would be received in the marketplace.

George showed up at my office with only a laptop computer and was ready to blow my mind with a program he claimed would level the playing field for individual day traders. According to George, his product contained a proprietary algorithm capable of thousands of calculations a second designed to tell someone when to buy or sell a stock. It dumbed down the process so much that all one had to do is watch the lights: if the light is green, buy a stock; if it's red, sell.

In December 1999, I had zero experience with using computers, but I thought, *Even I can do this.* The product had most of the ingredients I was looking for . . . or so I thought. When George attempted his first demonstration of the product, the software crashed. He blamed it on everything but the program. All I could think was, *Get this clown out of here.* In retrospect, it was kind of funny. But because I had a lot of time on my hands, I listened again, thinking, *What the hell have I got to lose?*

I felt bad for George. I believe everyone deserves a second chance, so I told him to call me once he got the kinks worked out. A week later, George called and asked if he could come see me. This time, when he turned on his computer, everything clicked just as he said it would. He had actually written and built a brilliant algorithm for trading stocks. His program made it easy for the average consumer to understand. Best of all, it worked! He called this ingenious product Wave on Wall Street. My knee began to bounce, as it does when I sense a winner. I remember thinking, *Kowabunga! The good Lord dropped this one smack dab in the middle of my lap!*

After we entered into a memorandum of understanding together, the next thing I did was enroll in a computer course at a local community college to learn how to turn on a computer. I didn't like the look of the original home page of the software, and so I drew what I wanted on a cardboard box using colored crayons. I also changed the name to Wizetrade. The outside of the box and the first user interface webpage were the most important to me. I knew everything else would follow suit once I designed those two elements. I knew nothing about writing software or even operating a computer, but I knew that if I could market the product and someone else could make sure it worked, then we'd have a winner.

Wizetrade (and its subsequent parent company, GlobalTec Solutions) became a huge success. I formed the company on

December 27, 1999. Four and a half years later, we had half a dozen complementary software products, several hundred thousand customers, recurring revenue (pure gold for an exit sale), and hundreds of associates. We were making money hand over fist and had amassed a couple hundred million dollars in annual revenue. We sold that company for a very respectable nine-figure sum. Wizetrade thrives today and is owned by a stock brokerage firm.

Don't waste time dwelling in self-pity about past mistakes. Get over it. We all make mistakes and nobody gives a flip. **They. Can't. Eat. You.** Life is about how you react to the mistakes that you will make. Wizetrade would have never happened had Unistar not crashed. I wouldn't be writing this book today and sharing what I have learned.

Passion and Happiness

My passion is building companies. It's what I do best. I'm a born builder who loves to create magical and wonderful enterprises from scratch—no office, no staff, and often no capital. Sometimes all I have had are good ideas and the perseverance to see them through. On our office wall in two of our buildings, we have a large mural that reads, "Faith, Passion, Tenacity, Focus, Monetization, Outrageous Sense of Urgency." That about says it all. I love to build products, sales teams, customer service teams, marketing plans, and creative cultures . . . everything it takes to raise a successful venture from the ground up. And as braggadocio as it may sound, I am good at it—*really* good. It's my blessing!

I have never aspired to become wealthy. Weird, huh? Counterintuitive? Not really—as long as I can live debt-free and pay my bills, I am really happy. To me, being rich is having a quality relationship with God and enjoying good health, a happy family, loyal friends, and freedom from debt (this means having my house and cars paid off as well). Happiness is also building a successful business from scratch, having the respect of my colleagues, having hundreds of happy staff members, and—of course—having thousands of satisfied customers. I don't consider myself a workaholic. I like to work at working smarter, not just working longer hours. Many people think they have to spend grueling days and sleepless nights to feel they are making a difference, but in the end, they are only making themselves miserable. Time in an office is not necessarily what it takes to be successful. Quality time at what you are doing is what it takes to be successful. Building successful companies is my passion. I'd rather be doing that than just about anything else—as long as it remains exciting when I ring the bell.

PART TWO

A Real Education

College Isn't Where You Learn the Business

This is important—and a bit controversial. It's crucial to have your eyes wide open on the subject of getting educated vs. simply growing up. I am not anti-education; I am simply a lot more pro-knowledge. Due to the lack of money in my family, and the fact that my parents did not go to college, my going to a university was never discussed in my household and wasn't an option for me. The only time I have been to a college was to see someone else graduate. Strangely enough, I have had hundreds of people tell me they would rather have had my path than the one they took through a college system. Looking at the big picture, I believe that college really serves one purpose: helping teenagers start maturing into adults. College is expensive and fun, but it won't guarantee you a job or give you assurance that you'll work in the field you studied. For most Americans, going to college in search of an education provides a colossally false sense of security and is a waste of money. Kids don't learn a lot of practical wisdom for the real world in many circumstances.

Ask a college student what he or she is studying sometime. Is he pursuing a business administration degree? Is she working on an advertising/marketing degree? Do students (and their parents) really believe they are going to learn those broad trades by being in a classroom and listening to a teacher who has very likely never been a business owner? Many instructors have never even worked in the professions they are teaching.

Much of the time, those kids don't even end up in their chosen field because once they graduate and discover what the real world is like, they are neither prepared nor truly educated enough to make it. Sadly, young adults today lack the skills needed to justify hiring them. Now, more than ever, there is a massive surplus of people with practical experience looking for work, so having a college degree doesn't mean as much to employers as genuine capability. Often, a certification is more valuable than a general college education. Most college students today are like zombies going through the motions. The good news is that dozens of wonderful higher learning organizations exist to give you the specific knowledge you need to succeed. For example, for social media marketing, you can get fully certified in about seven months by Splash Media University (www.SplashMediaU.com), and once you are certified, you can not only command a six-figure salary or drive your business with social media, but you can also add the accredited designation of CSMP to your business card. How bizarre is it that a guy (me) who has never been to college owns an accredited (by the Southern Association of Colleges and Schools) online university?

Remember, business owners can easily find skilled and knowledgeable workers to fill their positions . . . for the same amount of money they can hire a recent college graduate with nothing to offer but a B.S. degree in subjects such as fine arts or political science. Most college graduates today are simply not prepared for life when they get out of college—and they don't even know it.

Graduating from college is an accomplishment, but it isn't a preparation for what happens next. That is why I believe colleges and universities should be more concerned with teaching the basics, especially what to expect when you get into the workforce. For example, teach people exactly where the money goes when Uncle Sam takes federal, state, and unemployment taxes out of their paychecks. Teach students how the money is actually used once the government gets it.

For most kids, college is only important because it is the first time they are away from home, living on their own, and making their own decisions. The real benefit of college is the maturation that takes place and the bonding students experience with different types of people. Sadly, though, while the sorority or fraternity you pledged to might have mattered when you started school, it doesn't mean squat when you're interviewing for a job. Trust me, being the person who held your head over a toilet after every party isn't the mark of distinction that makes someone your friend for life.

"Really? How do you know?" you ask. "You didn't go to college, so how do you know?" I'm an authority because I have hired thousands of people, and in that time, I've seen it all.

I realize that some of you reading this page are wondering just about now if I'm out of my mind or simply justifying my position because I never went to college. The answer is neither. I may not have taken a traditional collegiate path, but I've definitely earned my Ph.D. in the actual business world. I've learned more from my losses than from my wins, and that is the kind of knowledge you will never get in a classroom.

But don't just take my word for it. A 2013 Gallup survey asked business leaders what they considered important in a job candidate's qualifications. Only 9 percent of employers said that the applicant's college location was "very important." Far more employers rated "knowledge of the field" (84 percent) and "applied skills in the field" (79 percent) as "very important."

Learning from Dad

Because I didn't go to college, I started on my road to success right out of high school. Success means having the courage, the determination, and the will to become the person you believe you were meant to be. I moved to Dallas, where I began my career working with my dad in the wholesale furniture business. I had $120 in my pocket, a clean car that was paid for, and lots of dreams.

My dad is a great man. We haven't always had a perfect relationship, but we love each other very much. We have walked different paths along the way, but there is no doubt in my mind that he gave me the work ethic I have today. Oddly, we don't have to talk much to understand each other. One day, however, when I was about twenty-two, my dad looked me in the eye and said, "Son, you have it all. You are going to be something big someday." I grinned and thanked him but didn't really know what he was talking about. My dad wasn't one to toss out statements like that unless he really meant it. Clearly, his statement stuck with me. It's funny how parents can say just one little thing that we never forget.

By the time I was twenty, I was on the road as a wholesale furniture manufacturer's representative. Dad and I split up his territory, with me taking southern and eastern Texas, Louisiana, and Arkansas as my three main areas of concentration; the rest of the territory was his. Like my dad, I would get in my car on Sunday night or early Monday morning and hit the road, selling my goods nonstop until late Thursday or Friday. We mostly serviced high-end furniture stores, so the orders were lucrative and plentiful. Although I was working predominantly on commission, I was making a good living for a kid right out of high school.

Week in and week out, I'd plan my time and set my schedule to maximize each itinerary. I spent more time building my relationships with the buyers than actually selling, because once they knew and trusted me, the sale was easy. Selling was fun. Everyone should experience selling something in his or her career because the feeling of closing a fat sale is unforgettable. When I knew I was about to close a sale, whether large or small, my knee would always begin to bounce. I took enormous pride each and every time I filled out an order form because I had something my customers needed, and it made me feel great to provide it to them. That thrill has not dissipated over the years. Every close really is like my first. Today I have the thrill of selling companies that I build, but it's the same feeling I got when I sold truckloads of furniture.

My father and I were selling the same furniture, but our lines were extremely different than our competitors' offerings, which is why we were wildly successful. Plus, we both had passion for our wares. We genuinely liked the products, so our enthusiasm was natural, authentic, and infectious. I don't believe I had a single customer who ever felt sold.

Selling Enthusiasm and Confidence

No matter what you are doing, you are always selling. You will see those words a lot throughout this book, but it is one of the most important lessons I can impart upon you as you enter the real world. Do whatever you can to learn to sell!

We are all salespeople. Think about how many times a day you are trying to get your way with family members or your spouse. Selling is a part of our DNA that we must dial into. There are hundreds of books and seminars on the art of selling. If you are one of those who does not think you are a salesperson, after you finish this book, start reading everything you can on the art of persuasion (aka selling).

The president of the United States is selling 24/7. The president is selling Congress, the international community, and the voters . . . all day, every day. When you apply for a job, you are selling yourself.

Learn how to sell, and learn how to overcome objections. Practice selling, and when you think you are done, practice some more. To be a good salesperson, it doesn't really matter what you're selling as long as what you have is different and you possess confidence and have passion. Don't think you can run an independent donut store and go up against Dunkin' Donuts if you are selling the same kind of donuts. You won't make it. You have to be the store selling donuts on a stick. Maybe it's the same donut, but it's a different vehicle of delivery. Now that works!

In the highly competitive world of auto insurance, we used our family dog Sparky, a white West Highland Terrier, as our mascot to give our boring auto insurance product a lovable personality—something most people never equate with auto insurance. Sparky was Unistar's auto insurance safety dog. She was the face of our product. We had Sparky coloring books for the kids, stuffed Sparky plush toys, and a six-foot Sparky mascot suit that one lucky soul wore in front of each insurance agency during its grand opening. No one else had Sparky!

Enthusiasm and passion about your product are the best sales tools you will ever have in your toolbox. Enthusiasm is infectious! If you are fired up and believe in your product, you will be successful. Confidence and enthusiasm will go a long way, but you also need a special spin on your product. For any company to thrive, it must provide something different that will set it apart from the competition right from the start.

For example, if you are selling a product—say a mattress— then sell it. Talk about the benefits, the technology, the research, and the customer satisfaction, but never—and I mean never—tell someone to buy your product because it is your best seller.

Really? That's your best pitch? When a salesman says that to me, I instantly think, *How lazy! He has no idea what he is trying to sell me!* If that's all you've got, pack it in. Go home. Game over. I mean it. You are done. Selling is not your calling.

I don't care if everyone else who walks into your store and lies down on that mattress loves it. That doesn't matter to me. If my wife walks into a department store to buy a dress, she sure doesn't want to buy the number-one-selling dress that she will see on every other woman around Dallas. It's absurd. (The only time this approach works is when it comes to food. If a waiter tells you that the restaurant's number one entrée is the steak, or that everyone loves the summer harvest salad, you might want to follow suit.)

To sell effectively, you have to talk about your product as though you know it from the inside out. Don't blurt out everything all at once. Stop and take a breath. Take a moment or two and just observe—to a fault. I am the type of guy who can tell you everything about a room after I walk out the door. I see every last detail and store it in my brain. That kind of attention to your surroundings can be a real gift if you channel it right. Picking up on the smallest details helps me better understand who I am dealing with and selling to, as well as what their needs are. To this day, I won't conduct business with someone until I see his or her office. I want to feel the vibe in the offices of the people with whom I am doing business.

I have learned to smell confidence, success, chaos, or even disorganization simply by walking through an office and taking in the environment. It's like looking in someone's car when he doesn't expect it. The inside of a car will tell you volumes about an individual. If it's basically a trash can, you can bet he lives a freewheeling, lazy, chaotic life. If, however, the car's interior is pristine—as though he just drove it off the lot, always clean and well kept—then you can bank on that person being the same way in other areas of life.

Above all, when I worked in furniture sales, I learned to take the time to listen to my buyers when they talked. As Stephen Covey says, "Seek first to understand, then to be understood." I always tried to keep our dialogue focused on the product. If it veered into personal territory, I did everything I could to steer the conversation back to sofas, tables, and chairs. I was there to sell, and if I wasn't closing, I wasn't getting paid. I worked on straight commission, so my time was worth money. Know your product inside and out, and ensure you have a better mousetrap than any other out there or you may as well stay home and not bother getting out of bed.

Regardless of what else you choose to do or the style of selling you prefer, to close effectively, you have to find your ace in every transaction—that one line you can fall back on that you know will seal the deal every time. My line has always been going in with a "you can't refuse this product" attitude. I am as passionate about selling as I am about business, so closing has always come easily to me. When I tell everyone that our product is the greatest, I firmly believe it, and they ultimately buy through my infectious enthusiasm.

If you are genuinely enthusiastic and knowledgeable about your product, people will sense the authenticity in everything you say. You have to know what you are talking about, because babbling and repeating yourself will not work. There aren't many things worse than a salesman who doesn't know about his product or who doesn't believe in it enough to convince someone else that he or she can't live without it.

ORTHODOX PATH: Learn the bare minimum about your product, and try to sell it. Wonder why you can't sell anything, and then work on your pitch, increasing the likelihood of sounding like a seventy-year-old used car salesman.

SPARKS PATH: Become passionate about your product, and let the infectious enthusiasm sell it for you.

Learning Your ABCs

Too often when it comes time to close the sale, salespeople won't ask for an order. They will keep talking and talking but they won't close. I have a great friend who is a smart and engaging businessman, but he systematically refuses to close the sale on his own products. He is an exceptionally personable guy who will spend an hour talking about how beautiful your child is, the vacation you took your wife on, and anything else he can find to hold your interest—but he won't ask for the order. We laugh about it all the time. He is one of those salesmen who prefer that you ask him if you can place an order with him, as opposed to his taking the order from you. You cannot be effective in sales if you don't know your ABCs:

ALWAYS

BE

CLOSING

How many of you will make a sales call and simply forget to ask for the order? How many times have you hung up the phone angry because you didn't make that sale? Believe me, it happens, but it doesn't have to. The secret to closing is simple: Just ask. If you don't ask, you don't get!

When you really think about it, people are closing 24/7 and they don't even realize it. Sometimes they get off their game and forget their purpose, but in the end they're closing. If you're a parent, you know that kids are great negotiators. When your son asks to play ball with some friends across the street, but you tell him no because it's dinnertime, you're closing him on why he can't play right now. Someone is always being closed. Either people are closing you, or you are closing them. In life, you want to be the one closing the sale. Period.

No matter what you're doing, the end goal is to close the sale, even if it's in print. When you are developing copy for an ad in a newspaper, you want to be closing in that ad, especially if you don't have the marketing budget to brand your company the way a large corporation can. If you're Nike, you can spend millions of dollars to get people to recognize your brand by its swoosh logo. But if you're a company that can't afford the same type of marketing, you have to rely on your limited advertising to show your customers they can get "this" from "that." Being consistent with that approach in every arena—whether it's via the web, the newspaper, or some other collateral material—will help sell the product. Think of your ads as though you are having a conversation with your customer and you are now closing the sale.

(NOTE: When do you know you have officially closed a transaction? When the check clears, and *only* when the check clears.)

Education by Design

I'm a bit like a chameleon in my ability to change and adapt to new challenges. I discovered, much to my surprise, that I had a passion for interior design. My interest in developing both rooms and products is an extension of my love of building and was likely influenced by all of my time selling furniture in high-end showrooms. I always respected what I saw and appreciated the nuances of each setup. I can tell when someone worked hard on his or her display because the quality always showed. I can inherently do some design that has to be a gift from God because there's no other explanation for my having those skills. You can't teach taste. You can teach the mechanics of design, but you cannot teach good taste.

If you have a vision, you have to execute it. For example, when I get a picture in my mind of something, I can somehow see it all the way through to a finished product. It's like what I imagine an artist sees before he starts to paint or sculpt. If you can envision the end result—I mean really see it in your mind— you can get anything done. Some years after I married my wife Jane, we bought a ranch about two hours outside Dallas. It took fourteen real estate closings to assemble the 360 acres of raw land that we wanted. We had to build everything on our ranch. We cleared land, paved roads, installed power lines, laid down electrical wiring, constructed bridges, and established running water lines all before we could break ground on a single building on the property. But I knew what I wanted and was able to communicate that vision to the team of highly skilled workers who helped bring it to life.

People have described this gift as having the ability to see things in 3-D. That's a great analogy because I can look at everything and see its underlying structure as though I were looking at it through perfectly clear glass. Imagine playing three-dimensional chess on three different glass boards and seeing how every move can affect your next move and every move that follows. To me, life is a three-dimensional chessboard. Every movement provides a fluid, 3-D outlook on things. If all you see is straight up and down—just horizontal or vertical lines—you are certainly handicapped as an entrepreneur.

It's crucial for entrepreneurs to learn to build on every step in the process so they can successfully get products to market. Work out the kinks along the way if you have to, because a product on your shelf is worthless until it's sitting on someone else's shelf. Ideas aren't worth diddly-squat if you don't put in the effort to get them to market. You have to sweat and worry to be outrageously successful.

The first company I built and owned was a little manufacturing business I started when I was twenty-one. I was making two-inch-thick, clear acrylic desk/trophy novelty pieces that were cut in the shape of Texas. I also engraved these items with an individual's name or company name and logo. I exclusively promoted these items from one-third page color ads in *Texas Monthly* magazine and sold thousands of them.

By the early 1980s, I had come up with the idea to design and manufacture mirrored placemats. Yep . . . a 12" x 18" piece of quarter-inch glass mirror with the edges clipped off, and a half-inch bevel all the way around them. I sold hundreds of thousands of those placemats via direct marketing and through retailers such as The Horchow Collection, Neiman Marcus, and Bloomingdale's, among others. I couldn't make the placemats fast enough to keep up with the orders. It was a good product with a great spin. (Shipping turned out to be a bear, but with tenacity we figured it out.)

I liked designing so much that I got out of the wholesale business and opened a high-end retail furniture and home accessory store. I had my mind set on selling products that were unique and special. Soon, I was designing and manufacturing screens, home goods, mirrored furniture, and other home goods that became highly sought-after items for interior designers and their clients. Before I knew it, people were coming to me to decorate their homes and offices. (Remember: I do not have a degree in interior design. As I said earlier, you can't teach taste. I simply have tremendous passion . . . and passion conquers all.)

After doing commercial design work, it was a natural next step for me to start a commercial construction company. I became

THEY CAN'T EAT YOU

a general contractor who subcontracted all of the construction work necessary to finish my clients' spaces. This approach enabled me to control the costs and the profit. Clients came to me and said, "Here's my space; I need X number of offices and desks." I'd design, plan, and then build each space. I transferred my passion to build into those kinds of projects. Design was an unbridled passion I didn't realize I had, but as my projects grew, so did my interest and expertise. Where some guys might subscribe to *Sports Illustrated* or *Golf Magazine*, I subscribed to *Architectural Digest, Dwell, Interior Design* magazine, *USA Today,* and *Businessweek.* I could go into a large, raw space and turn it into a showroom floor just as easily as I could take an empty office and turn it into a state-of-the-art production facility. By the time I was twenty-seven, I had made my first million bucks. It was a milestone, but making a million dollars had never been my goal or my dream. Making money just happened through my passion and desire to succeed.

The Restaurant Business –
Another "Education"

One of my favorite projects during those years was the construction of my own restaurants. I think everyone should be in the restaurant business once in his or her life. "Hard work" is an understatement. I have tremendous respect for people who succeed in the restaurant industry.

My restaurant was called Pepper's. Yes, my business platform was to emulate the Chili's restaurant concept and put a new spin on it by adding a Tex-Mex menu (Chili's was all about burgers in those days). We were successful; we had a 220-seat, full-service restaurant and often had up to a forty-five minute wait at lunch. People regularly came in and said, "We are so glad to have a Chili's in the neighborhood." Emulating has its benefits, as I don't think there are too many new ideas out there; however, be careful not to flat-out copy another's idea or product. The late, great restaurateur Norm Brinker, of Steak and Ale and Chili's Grill & Bar fame, lived across the street from my first Pepper's restaurant and—after coming in for months and sharing glorious, kind words about our food, service, and atmosphere—he called me over one day and said, "Son, I love what you are doing; however, you know I have to sue you."

I said, "What?"

He replied, "I can't let you copy me to this degree." He (his in-house lawyers) sent me a nice but firm letter and demanded that I change my name and my menu. I was able to make the changes just enough to make them happy. WHEWWWWWW! It was an expensive lesson but worth it.

(NOTE: Don't "emulate" anything too closely because if you are successful, those whom you "copied" might end up owning your business!)

We had lots of fun, but it was by far the hardest work I have ever done. It was a seven-day-a-week proposition. I worked long hours and, as an entrepreneur, experienced lots of frustration. Most of the staff was made up of flakey drifters who jumped from one restaurant job to the next without giving me, or the poor guy I got them from, any notice. They were challenging to manage because, for the most part, they were there to collect a paycheck, meet girls (or guys), and move on. They weren't interested in making a career out of being a server or bartender. Even so, I found that running a restaurant came quite naturally to me, so I opened a second one.

I can walk into nearly any business and manage it the same way regardless of the product—chicken wings or wingback chairs, it's all the same to me. Even my philanthropic cause, The Samaritan Inn, is a business—it's just the business of helping people get back on their feet.

Even though I didn't know much about the day-to-day operation of a restaurant, I was smart enough to hire a manager who did—from Chili's, of course! Many business owners make the mistake of handing the reins over to someone else and remaining virtually absent. That isn't how I approach a new endeavor. While I entrusted my business to this manager, I also used him as my coach so I could learn everything necessary to keep things operational in case he left or I had to assume those responsibilities myself for any reason.

I spent two years nurturing those locations until one day I had had enough. The restaurants were a detour—a distraction from my crumbling first marriage and a way to reinvent myself into something new and different. I made a good living during those years, but truth be told, I didn't want to just make a good living. I wanted to do something really big. I wasn't going to do it with restaurants. I started pruning. It was time to get out, so I sold the restaurants and my retail home goods store, and I began to throw my entire focus into building my commercial construction business. I didn't realize at the time that this business was morphing into an insurance company due to the relentless necessity for insurance and surety bonding.

There was one unforgettable and surprising benefit to being in the restaurant business that would change the course of my life forever. It was there that I met my wife Jane, the love of my life. She was dating one of my bartenders, and I was just finalizing my divorce from a twelve-year marriage to my high school sweetheart. At first it didn't occur to me that Jane and I could be a "thing." I certainly wasn't ready to date, and she was seeing someone else.

Still, the more we got to know one another, the more the "Sparks" flew. Jane and I eventually began to date and, twenty-eight years later . . . it's all good!

ORTHODOX PATH: Constantly reinvent the wheel.

SPARKS PATH: Emulate success, rinse, and repeat!

PART THREE

Finding and Funding Your Dream

I have often been asked how I achieve financial success without a stake or capital to start my businesses. This is a great question, and unless you have a rich aunt, there is only one way to do it. You have to save your nickels and dimes and invest in your dream yourself. I like to equate it to my days playing baseball. I had to hit thousands of baseballs before I was able to hit one out of the park. But once I figured out how to do it, I became the cleanup batter (number four) and always swung for the fence! Pitchers started walking me because they knew if I connected, it was game over. However, make no mistake . . . no one has ever hit a baseball over the fence on his first swing at bat. Base hits are a very good thing to get ready for the exhilaration and success of a home run. Plan on hitting a lot of base hits first!

Hungry Entrepreneurs

To me, there are five stages to the skeleton of any new business:

1. Starting
2. Surviving
3. Building
4. Thriving
5. Exiting (selling or merging)

So how do you begin? I'll share a real-life, step-by-step example of how to fund your dream without a dime to your name. Let's say you want to be a residential real estate developer.

1. First get a job at a residential real estate development company. Don't worry about the job or the pay. You are there to get educated, not to get rich.

2. Learn everything you can. Beg the boss to let you sit in on meetings (showing enthusiasm is a good thing with your new employer, too). It's amazing what you will pick up just by exposure.

3. Take on every odd job the company will give you. Ask daily if you can do anything else to help.

4. Get your residential real estate agent license at night and weekends. (Your employer will be impressed again!)

5. Scour the market for a piece of real estate; low income areas are great for fixer-uppers. Your goal is to just get one under your belt. Save enough to put just a few dollars down and get the owner to finance the rest for about three years (with a balloon payment due in three years) and tell him that you will put in all the sweat equity to fix it up (paint, woodwork, cleaning, yard work).

I did this several times when I was getting started. I didn't have a pot to piss in or a window to throw it out of, but I did it. All you need is a credit card and a Home Depot. The guy with whom I negotiated to buy my first properties was lazy. His weakness was my strength. The rent from the duplex (both sides) paid the monthly payments and left a few dollars so I could constantly upgrade the property. The renters received a Section 8 housing subsidy from Uncle Sam, and that guaranteed I would get my rent payments from them. I ended up selling the two duplexes for an $87,000 profit in just nineteen months. I did, however, leave a few drops of blood on the property when I was changing out the windows.

ORTHODOX PATH: Admit defeat because you don't have any capital to get started. Submit to the fact that you have a J.O.B., and that's all you'll ever have.

SPARKS PATH: Get a job in the industry you are passionate about, and submerse yourself in the business while saving just enough nickels to go out on your own the minute the opportunity arises (and the opportunity *will* arise).

You can do this with any business idea. Donut shops (I hear they make serious money, too) or software . . . it doesn't matter. Get a job and submerse yourself in the industry you want a piece of; seize the opportunity when you feel like you have graduated and the iron is hot.

Cash or capital alone does not ensure your success. Billions of dollars have been tossed at ideas that never got off the ground. Fire in the belly, tenacity, and a cold hard desire to win ensures success. Years later, I still look for the guys with fire in their bellies and an insane desire to win. I never toss money at an entrepreneur and say, "Good luck!"

Statistically, only one out of ten entrepreneurs has the ability to succeed when he or she is tossed a bag of cash. All of the entrepreneurs in which I invest are submersed into our system. I was that entrepreneur once, and I know what they need ... which is way beyond cash. They need legal assistance, accounting, bookkeeping, information technology (IT), intellectual property (IP), graphic arts, websites, marketing expertise, synergistic connections, office space, warehouse space, software programming, sales expertise, human resources, fulfillment expertise, and coaching and mentoring. I have learned to provide the entrepreneurs I invest in with exactly what they need to succeed, and that is why I win more often than I lose. I stack the deck.

Time and Money

People often ask me what I like to invest in as a serial entrepreneur. I think this is a great question, as my answer telegraphs volumes of information.

My time is actually more valuable to me than my money is. Invariably, I am compelled along the journey to put in a little sweat and blood on each venture. So far, I have never been able to get my time back once I have spent it. I am extremely careful not to get sucked into an investment that completely engulfs my time and my human capital (my brain). It sounds like a simple proposition, right? Not so fast! Trust me, if you are into an investment that is going south, it is human nature to give it 100 percent of your total attention as you try to make it succeed.

The most important advice I can give an entrepreneur is this: never bring me an opportunity that a third grader can't understand. Yep, a third grader! Every single, challenging transaction of mine started because, from the beginning, I had never completely understood the product.

I'm not comparing myself to Warren Buffett by any stretch of the imagination, but have you ever looked at his portfolio of assets at Berkshire Hathaway? Let me help you:

- Coca-Cola (soft drinks)
- Gillette (razor blades)
- GEICO (auto insurance)
- Dairy Queen (ice cream and cheeseburgers)
- Mars (candy bars)
- See's Candies (candy)
- Heinz (ketchup)
- Fruit of the Loom (underwear)
- Justin Brands, Inc. (boots)
- Nebraska Furniture Mart (furniture)
- Acme Brick (bricks)
- Kansas Bankers Surety Co. (surety bonds)
- Burlington Northern Santa Fe Railway (trains)

There are many others, but you get the idea. I have no idea how to make razor blades, but the point is that the majority of the people need and want a razor blade. The public uses nearly everything listed in Warren Buffett's multibillion-dollar portfolio.

I took a page from Warren's book; however, the difference between Warren and me (other than his billions of dollars) is that he acquires companies, and I build companies from scratch. For both of us, the fundamentals are exactly the same: KISS. "Keep It Simple, Stupid."

Marc Sparks's private equity investments of time and money (to name a few):

- Cardinal Telecom, LLC (national cell retail distribution)
- Consolidated Surety (surety bonds)
- Unistar (auto insurance)
- Agency Matrix (auto insurance office management software)
- Reliant Healthcare (rehabilitation hospitals)
- Blue Jay Wireless (cell phones and service provider)
- Boxstar (ads on labels on boxes)
- Wizetrade and Options Made Easy (trading software with red and green lights)
- TSTN – The Success and Training Network (life skills training)
- Splash Media University (accredited online university)

I primarily gravitate toward products and services that can be sold to thousands or millions of customers. I do this because I know I can out-package and out-market anyone if given the chance to do so. Remember, before GEICO had the lizard, Unistar had Sparky the Safety Dog.

ORTHODOX PATH: Invest in super-complicated products that only a handful of people can buy.

SPARKS PATH: Stay the course! Invest your time and money in products designed for the masses . . . products that can be explained easily in three words or fewer.

Think about it; we are all a bunch of struggling working stiffs just trying to make it to the next day and win in the battle of life and business. The only way to be sure that happens is to be the best at what you do—or at least make people think you are the best.

One of the ways I've been able to fake it 'til I made it over the years, aside from overeducating myself on whatever it is I am selling, is to be smart and humble enough to bring in talented people who really know what they're doing in their fields of expertise.

Confidence and passion conquer all! Become a master at your product or service, and you will sell more than anyone else because you are the most confident person in the room.

Before starting Splash Media, I had often hired a certain production company to create video elements for the seminars we hosted to promote Wizetrade and to work on the companion training DVDs. That is how I met Chris Kraft, an award-winning director and producer who specialized in video training and who owned the production company we used. Over the course of four and a half years, he and I worked together on several projects. During that time, I really got to know Chris. I trusted him, believed in him, and was absolutely sold on his ability to deliver a high-quality product on time and within the budgets we set.

Chris came to me with the idea of building a state-of-the-art television production studio, where we could cultivate a community among users of Wizetrade. He envisioned a mechanism that would allow our customers to communicate with each other. At the time, we were already producing online audio programs in the form of web-based streaming talk shows; from this, we decided to take our streaming audio shows and adapt them for live TV. We called it TTV (Traders Television Network) and imagined it to be something like a version of CNN, but with a focus on investing and trading. TTV would also promote the Wizetrade and Options Made Easy software tools we had developed.

When I first heard Chris's pitch, I wasn't interested. My attention had been on building Wizetrade and its parent company, GlobalTec Solutions. Since the company's inception with its flagship Wizetrade software program, which had revolutionized the way traders trade stocks, we had expanded the product line to include several more programs. Options Made Easy was a software program specifically designed for option traders. 4X Made Easy software connected and empowered investors with the latest online technological tools, including real-time currency-price-trending analysis. Commodities Made Easy provided individual traders unparalleled access to trade commodities and futures. The Command TRADE software was designed to back-test investment strategies against historical data so traders could automate their trading portfolios through an integrated broker partner. By the time I sold the company in June 2004, we had several hundred staff members, over 200,000 users of our software programs, and hundreds of millions of dollars in revenue, all from an idea conceived in the back bedroom of Wizetrade's originator, George Thompson.

I had certainly made enough money by that time to retire. But you see, I'm not that guy. After the sale of GlobalTec Solutions, it took me about a day or so (literally) before I called Chris and said, "You remember that idea you had? Let's do it!" After being a top video production vendor of mine for four and a half years, Chris and I joined forces under the same umbrella. I acquired his production company, and that was how we started Splash Media.

The goal was to build a state-of-the-art "live" television studio on the burgeoning Splash Media campus. I didn't know anything about production or the technology it takes to build a cutting-edge production facility, but I knew that Chris did. I was certain that if we built it, they would come, and so we did. Chris needed a functional space where he'd be able to create high-quality video content. We took 4,000 square feet of raw real estate located on the ground floor of a predominantly residential building. There were exposed pipes and plumbing everywhere and, to most, it would have been a logistical nightmare. The sound of flushing toilets and running water is the last thing you want to hear in a live television studio—we had our work cut out for us from the start.

We got the two most talented studio designers in Dallas to come on board. Over the course of the past twenty years, they had arguably built the best production facilities in Dallas. They were experienced and smart and would help us build our dream. Chris and I walked through the space with our project engineer, discussing every detail—from the ceilings, which I was told were too low; to the floors, which didn't have any sound insulation; to the walls, which were way too tight for cameras. Pipes would have to be rerouted and the space practically gutted and refitted to pull this off. The project manager thought it would take eighteen months or more to design, build, and complete the job. I said, "Ahhh . . . but you can get it done in six or less!"

Moving at Sparks Speed

This is a good place to explain to you what everyone around me has dubbed Sparks Speed. For as long as I can remember, the normal time and space continuum under which the average person operates has not existed for me. If I make a decision to do something, I'm all in. This means compressing the amount of time it usually takes into a far more efficient timeframe. I do this so I can get my idea up and running while others are still laboriously talking it through. We are going to make mistakes, and I'd rather make those mistakes now than make them tomorrow.

There is a cost of working at this accelerated pace, both in a financial regard and in staying power. I definitely spend a lot more money moving at this pace, but I also get our products and services to market much faster. The lost opportunity cost of not doing something is much greater than the mistakes you make when executing quickly.

The amount of money we were going to spend on the studio never scared me. Chris is a pragmatic individual, but I am a dreamer who was willing to just do it. My just do it approach to business makes people accountable because it forces them to follow through. I'm a "But what if we could get a 100,000 happy customers paying us $99 a month now?" kind of guy. I see it in 3-D, and then I do it. That difference between Chris and me—his practical nature and my active optimism—is what makes the ebb and flow of our relationship work so well to this day.

Art Williams is a self-made man and motivational speaker who gives one of the most commanding speeches I've ever heard. He inspires me every time I hear it. It's called "Just Do It." The talk is an example of Art's philosophy on winning in business, and he ought to know. After giving up his career as a high school football coach, Art went on to build a multibillion-dollar insurance business based on the idea that customers buy term life insurance instead of whole life insurance and invest the difference they save in the process. His company ultimately employed 150,000 people and sold more insurance than Prudential and New York Life—the number one and two companies—combined. He had a vision and the entrepreneurial spirit to "Just Do It." If you want to be truly inspired, Google "Art Williams' Just Do It" speech and watch it on YouTube.

If you persevere and are committed to your vision, the things that present themselves as challenges will often become something spectacular—if they are handled correctly along the way. Sometimes my expectations burn people out before a project is finished, but at the end of the day, it will get done. Despite the costs and occasional casualties, Sparks Speed works.

Have you ever noticed that you get ten times as much done just days before you head out on vacation than on most other days? Everyone knows that frantic but exciting get-it-done speed you travel at when you have to clear the decks for a week or so out of the office. That's Sparks Speed! We operate at that pace every day, on every project, for every company. Sparks Speed is our culture and one of the secret weapons we use to achieve our success. We are first to market, first to make mistakes, first to make corrections . . . and first to revenue.

You usually get one shot at winning a customer, and if your sales process, customer service, follow-through, or even your shipping is anything less than great, then you most likely will suffer the consequences of a cancelation or return. That's what seeing things in 3-D in business looks like. It's having the ability to visualize the outcome—the finished product—long before it's ever built.

Our original plan for Splash Media was to build three separate television studios, something that would prove a nearly impossible challenge because of the space we were committed to. We also needed an environment in which we could create programming—our own as well for our clients—as we always retained the option of renting the space out. From the start, we had a huge wish list of features that would make our studio different from and better than all the others . . . like that good ol' donut on a stick!

Much of the technology we wanted to include had never been put together before. This technology included special flat-panel screen displays, which had to be handmade, and a computer network that provided production and audio functions from any seat in the control room. We even hired a programmer to create software for one of the custom pieces we designed and built so that one of the cameras could move across the X and the Y axes robotically. The company that manufactured the camera for us had never seen this before, so they created a new design while we came up with the interface to make it work. We wanted the space to be flexible enough to accommodate any scenario. We created this vision on the fly. There were no plans until we laid it out for the designers. Our specs may have been challenging, but they were also half the fun.

While we were busy with general construction of our television studio, I was simultaneously working with our in-house graphics designer to create a brochure and website around our business model. The stationery and brochures are always tied to the look and feel of the website, which is tied to the look and feel of the product and the facility. We were barely under construction, yet we were working on collateral support components.

Why? Because I wanted people to see the vision I saw. I needed them to grasp that we were building the most techno-logically advanced studio in Texas, if not the entire country. The brochure was a tool to help create buzz around the studio and our concept, long before we were finished. As the studio evolved, so did the website and collateral material (the marketing brochure). We printed several editions over the course of the six months of construction. Compared to the cost of the studio, the website and brochure were inexpensive and effective marketing tools that couldn't have been overused.

Every new business should strive to eke out at least a tiny profit in its FIRST year. I found it vital to the momentum and moral of the core team to see the fruits of your labor . . . plus, it keeps the repo man at bay!

We started the construction of our $5.2 million studio in December 2004 and were open and ready for business six months later, in June 2005. It was a 24/7 proposition to meet the goal. There were a few glitches along the way, but this is where faith stepped in. Most people are programmed to tell you why you can't do something, but discouragements don't stop us from forging ahead. Everyone on the team was working concurrently to ensure the space we were building could accommodate the millions of dollars of custom-designed equipment.

I am a grow-fast guy. Many companies are happy taking a three-to five-year path to build their reputation in the marketplace and to roll out a traditional growth plan. I don't work that way. I build companies to sell them within four to five years. I always start with an exit strategy and often with the buyer targeted! After all, "They can't eat you!" The days of building a business and passing it down to your children are just about over. If you're successful, private equity firms or synergistic buyers will come in and make you an offer you won't likely refuse, and you will eventually sell anyway.

It has never mattered much to me whether I knew about a business I wanted to be involved in before I invested. I had zero experience in owning a restaurant when I opened Pepper's. I absolutely loathed the stock market when I cofounded Wizetrade, which ultimately became GlobalTec Solutions. I didn't even know how to use a computer when I was selling that software program.

I knew nothing about production when I built our television studio, but you can bet it didn't take me long to understand that business enough to sound like I knew what I was talking about.

ORTHODOX PATH: Develop a five-, ten-, and fifteen-year road map for your business.

SPARKS PATH: Start with the goal of selling your business in three years. Focus on that target with every single decision you make, every single day.

PART FOUR

Fifty Sparks

Sometimes all it takes is a spark to start a raging fire. It is my hope that you will read the following "Sparks" and apply them to your own entrepreneurial journey. Apply them all and don't look back. Don't be afraid! I'll see you in the winner's circle!

Invest in the Person, Not the Company

To get my attention, I must first have an interest in the idea. Second, I need to believe in the person behind the product—its "face." Simply put, I want to know everything about the people with whom I go into business. Who are they? How tenacious do they appear to be? Do I like them personally? Can I spend time with them?

I want to know about their goals in life. I want to take rides in their cars and see how they keep them. If a vehicle is a disaster, they will clearly get a demerit! If it is organized and spotless and looks like I could eat off the floor, then their stock goes up with me. I hope to hear that they have failed a few times along the way because that tells me they are persistent, like a dog with a bone. I'm looking for a burning hot fire in the belly. Do you still have passion for what you are doing, even though you've failed at it previously? I don't believe an entrepreneur can fully understand success or what it is to be burning hot to succeed without first having experienced failure. Failure makes us hungry. It keeps us competitive and humble.

When I first met George Thompson, before agreeing to fund, mentor, and incubate his trading software idea, I put him through a rigorous personality profile test and compared it with mine. According to this test, we were a perfect match for collaborating on ventures. The consultant who conducted the test said he had never seen two people so well-suited for working together in business. And he was dead on. George had his strengths and weaknesses, and I had mine. We fed off of one another. It's a rare find, but extremely valuable. We had a successful run with Wizetrade.

4–10 Startup Plan

One way to fund a great idea or company without capital is what I call my 4–10 startup plan. Give 10 percent of the equity of your new company to the four key individuals who matter most:

1. Lawyer
2. Accountant or Bookkeeper
3. Director of Marketing and Sales
4. Webmaster or Graphic Designer

Of course you have to sell these key individuals on your vision; however, that too will provide you with valuable kernels of wisdom to succeed once you have accomplished your initial startup goal. Just discussing the idea of the 4–10 Startup Plan often brings up other individuals who will love to help support your idea. Once this is done, all you have to do is identify one of your new partners' offices that you can use, and hang out your shingle to let the world know you are in business.

Power of Synergy

Synergy can be a massively successful force when played right. Two plus two can easily equal ten if you pair the right parties. I once invested in a great entrepreneur who had everything I look for in the face of a product. He had passion, seasoning, intelligence, the power of persuasion, a killer resume, street smarts, and finally—best of all—he had lots of scars yet still had fire in his belly. He came to me wanting to build state-of-the-art rehabilitation hospitals. He wanted to build and run sixty-bed rehab hospitals for patients who were just leaving the hospital after a stroke or an orthopedic surgery, such as on knees, hips, or shoulders. The challenge here was that the cost to get in the game was really high. A single sixty-bed rehabilitation hospital can cost $20 million to build and require $6 million to $8 million in operating capital. And all of these requirements were in an economy when it was impossible to get ten cents out of a bank.

I decided to put two and two together, and I introduced my brilliant rehabilitation entrepreneur to a hard-charging, take-no-prisoners kind of commercial construction developer ... and the rest is history. All we had to do was build a who's who cast of rehabilitation-experienced resumes for our first hospital and marry our operations guys with my developer's talent for commercial properties, and all of a sudden, as a team, we were bankable. The companies were separate, but my developer needed a talented, twenty-year tenant so he could get the loan to build the buildings, and my operator needed a building in which to operate his rehabilitation hospitals. Once I assembled the dream team, I jumped at the chance to be the primary catalyst (investor) on both sides of the transaction, and it felt as though I were conducting my own symphony orchestra. We built several hospitals in half a dozen cities and sold the company and the real estate for millions of dollars. And none of it would have happened had we not put two and two together synergistically.

ORTHODOX PATH: Run each company separately and flounder.

SPARKS PATH: Run each company in concert to maximize each company's strengths as an interdependent unit.

Establish Good Habits

I am a habitual person by nature, and I define integrity by what people do when no one else is watching. Every morning, I wake up, turn on the coffeemaker, and spend about fifteen minutes reading some form of devotional scripture while standing up. I never sit in the morning until I get to my office. (For gosh sakes, I have just been in bed for the past seven and a half hours!) I know to my core that I am a conduit for God, and this daily routine puts me on point for what really matters in my life. Next, I read *The Dallas Morning News* to catch up on current events and, of course, for marketing inspiration. I then drop to the floor and really wake up by doing thirty military-style pushups to get the blood flowing. You might be surprised that doing just thirty pushups can impact your day. I don't always want to do it, but I know that once I'm done I feel great! I spend about ten minutes doing some cardiovascular activity (treadmill or elliptical). By the time I finish my wake-up routine, I am ready and eager to start my day. BOOYAH!

If you wake up in a bad mood, stressed out, or with a case of the blues, this short morning routine will help turn your day around before it gets started. It gives me confidence and clarity and the feeling that I can move mountains and create miracles.

I created this habit and turned it into a regular morning routine because I know that I always set the tone in my office. If I walk in tired, rundown, hungover, or out of shape, that sends a message to everyone else, and it ultimately dictates what I get back from them. But if I walk in with a sense of invigorating energy, I know they will feed off it. If for some reason I get a temporary lull in my energy during the day, I take a five-minute power nap to reinvigorate myself. I simply kick off my shoes, remove my watch, and lie down on the floor. I've always had the ability to fall asleep in the midst of chaos, so I can take power naps almost anywhere. There's great value in closing your eyes when needed, so long as this habit doesn't turn into a daily routine or last longer than a couple of minutes.

I also make it a point to get in a full workout three out of seven afternoons in any given week. Luckily, there is a gym on the campus near our offices, so I don't have to go very far. I usually take printouts of emails or paperwork with me to read on the treadmill (a tricky feat I mastered so I wouldn't cause bodily injury to myself). Even then, I am using that time to get informed and to get ahead. More important, I am setting an example for everyone else regarding the value of taking care of oneself. If I am not taking care of myself—if I am living a hard life, boozing it up, smoking, and eating horrible food—then I am committing what I see as the cardinal sins that prevent you from ever winning.

Why? People around me are looking for direction and influence. If I am out of shape, they won't respect me. Think about an overweight politician. If he can't take care of himself, how will he ever take care of his constituency? You wouldn't take heart or diet advice from an obese doctor. You wouldn't want beauty advice from someone who doesn't take care of her appearance. Why would you take business advice from someone you don't look up to and respect? As an entrepreneur or leader, you can't expect people to listen to your advice and ignore your example. What you create as a habit for yourself can easily and quickly become routine for others.

I was thirty-two, and about a year after I started what would morph into Unistar. One day, I realized that I had a degenerative disc in my lower back. The damn thing hit me like a ton of bricks . . . one day I'm a happy-go-lucky, hard-charging entrepreneur, and the next I am flat on my back. I would not let the pain and suffering affect Unistar's progress, so I rented a hospital bed and had it brought to my office. I placed it against the window across from my desk, and when I got to the office each morning, I would simply lie down there so we didn't skip a beat.

The only solution to my lower back pain was to strengthen the muscles around the degenerative disc so the muscle would take the workload away from the disc. Guess how I had to get the muscle built up? Yep . . . exercise! Oh my gosh, I can still hear my screams from my walking on a treadmill at a 15 percent incline each day. Within a few months, I was able to remove the hospital bed and move on with my life; however, this is what got me in the routine of my wake-up workouts. Funny how life has a way of getting your attention to get you to do what you should have been doing all along.

ORTHODOX PATH: Drink a few cups of coffee, take a shower, and go to the office.

SPARKS PATH: Drink a few cups of coffee, spend two minutes in prayer and devotional, read the local newspaper, and do twenty pushups, twenty jumping jacks, and ten minutes on an elliptical.

The Optimal Work Environment

Most of the people around me think I have a slight form of Obsessive Compulsive Disorder (OCD). To be fair to my family and friends who may be reading this book, I think we can all agree that I probably do have some form of OCD, peppered with a wee bit of Attention Deficit Disorder. However, I choose to embrace my peculiarities. It's true that I like things a certain way, and, yes, I am somewhat of a neat freak. To me, a cluttered desk is a cluttered mind! I require consistency and the discipline for consistency in my associates, right down to the smallest detail, including the size of the paper clips we use in the office. Who invented the little paper clips anyway? No little ones for me; only the jumbo size will do. I don't like it when people hand me an important document and it has a cute little pink paper clip binding it. This tells me you think what we're doing is whimsical and really not that important. The small paper clips are usually just a waste of metal, as they don't hold more than two pieces of paper, so why bother? I also don't believe in people's decorating their cubicles and turning them into shrines to their favorite rock star, college, friends, and pets. What's worse is that the items in these shrines usually end up surrounded by half-dead plants starved for the sunlight they need to survive. Remember, perception is reality.

What if a VIP client walks through your workspace and experiences your shrine to the "University of Who Gives a Damn" when he happens to be an Oklahoma fan? That might be just the thing to make him change his mind about doing business with your company. I know that when I tour someone else's headquarters, I am there to observe. Everything.

When I go to anyone's office, you can bet I am looking for clues the way that Lieutenant Columbo used to. I'm looking beyond the obvious so I can see inside the lives of the people who run the day-to-day operations. I want to know who they are, right down to the smallest detail. Trust me; office cubicles are a great place to start your own internal investigation. It would be so much easier to just tell my staff to knock themselves out decorating their spaces, but that would be like telling children not to clean their rooms.

ORTHODOX PATH: Staff runs amok in their workspace.

SPARKS PATH: Establish a professional look and feel that expresses the image you want to portray, and empower your associates to become the ambassadors.

In our offices, the code allows for one personal photograph and one other personal item on your desk. That's it. You're at work. You're not in your living room. At the end of the day, our associates are being paid a good wage to do a good job. As a business owner, you want everyone to stay focused on what he or she is there to do to be successful. I want everyone devoted to the business—not to shrine building. Coming to work isn't the same as going to a party. The atmosphere must be completely professional, or you risk its becoming something else less appealing to your clients. Holding firm to these types of limits keeps that separation clear. So many people come to work thinking, *It's time to establish my work family.* I find it the notion of a family at an office a bit disturbing. You are supposed to be a high-performing team, more like a sports team that rewards those who perform. A business will fail miserably if employees think they are at Aunt Mary's for a birthday party instead of on a field of battle each day. I'm not saying don't enjoy your business environment at all; in fact, I believe that laughter is great medicine for ironing out the challenges of a day. You gotta laugh!

After more than three decades of building companies and the cultures within those companies, I found that the team is far more productive and happier with solid ground rules established about their environment. I found that people really have no desire to work in an environment that resembles a chaotic fraternity house gone amok. People desire structure where their bread is buttered.

> "Setting a philosophy and being explicit about it is scary. You can easily have fears about becoming stagnant or irrelevant. But it's important to provide a North Star—to provide an anchor."
>
> —Julia Hartz

The other day, I was reading an article in *Inc.* magazine, "Who Needs a Happy Work Force? This Works Better." Eventbrite cofounder Julia Hartz described exactly what I have been saying for years: quite a few high-performing companies have poor workplace cultures, while some companies deemed the "best places to work" experience lackluster performance. Hartz explained that when she and her team set goals and clear expectations for her own company, Eventbrite, the business improved. She refocused the developers on core products and tasked the service team with creating better experiences for their customers. As a result, Eventbrite's engineering team grew by 30 percent, the company posted $2 billion in gross ticket sales in 2013, and their attrition rate was only 5 percent.

When I read this, I thought, *Finally! Solid data my theory is right!* At the end of the day, no one works for an employer because he has a ping-pong table in the lobby or brings in a back massager once a month . . . or even for the occasional free lunch or Christmas party. I have never heard an employee say, "I really should stay because he throws a hell of a party each year." I have done everything you can think of to keep staff happy (so I thought), but a few years ago I found that people just want to be slightly overpaid for what they do, and if they feel respected (praised), you keep them for life. All the rest is just noise!

If you are struggling with associates using social media for personal reasons or outside of their scope of work, you don't have a Facebook or Twitter problem, you have a work ethic problem. Before the Internet, these were the same type of staff members who hung around the watercooler, making personal phone calls or playing

computer solitaire all day long. If you have associates who have become experts at wasting time, their choice of venue is irrelevant. They aren't productive members of your team. This is simply office complacency cancer, and you must remove it immediately. Banning the use of Facebook or Twitter and other such sites won't solve your problem because those people will always find an outlet to waste time (theirs and yours) on the job. You need to address the problem and not the symptom. My suggestion is to cut them loose—and fast. Leopards don't change their spots!

Never ever forget that all people in your organization are selling. It doesn't matter where they sit or with whom they come into contact, they are sending a message on your behalf. Many times the only person, other than you, that a client might come into contact with is the receptionist. That makes him or her one of the most important members of your team. Many entrepreneurs fail without even realizing it because they have a lackluster, unengaged person at the front desk. The front desk person is your best foot forward! A humdrum individual at your front desk reveals to visitors, "I don't care what you think," or, "I'm cheap and I can't afford an A-Teamer to represent me," or, "I cut corners, and we don't have a quality product!" It also says you are not quality driven. A happy, professional, energetic receptionist in an office is so refreshing. When I walk into someone else's office and am greeted by someone with these attributes, it instantly communicates that the company cares about me and confirms why I am in that office. A quality person at the front desk will be selling without selling as well—he or she telegraphs success and confidence. A really strong receptionist can also diffuse an otherwise agitated situation. Always bear in mind that a quality receptionist is your first chance to win over a new customer.

These may seem like ridiculous, tiny details, but once you let go of these kinds of office codes, things have a way of snowballing. Keeping them in place creates healthy habits and consistency among the team. At first, new staff members are a little taken back, but eventually they become ambassadors to the code and rally toward for the greater good of the vision.

ORTHODOX PATH: Hire an inexpensive receptionist.

SPARKS PATH: Hire a professional, experienced executive assistant to work the reception desk, and empower him or her to represent your company as you would.

What Gets Written, Gets Done

One of the most important habits I've developed is to create a weekly to-do list that helps me prepare for the coming week. Even though I have moved into a technological world with the use of my laptop, iPad, and iPhone, I still choose to handwrite my to-do list old-school style because real magic takes place between your brain and the pen in your fingertips. Handwriting your list creates an unforgettable mental connection. This type of connection is intentional; it establishes a conscious awareness of the things you want to accomplish. I find that by physically writing things down, I rarely forget them, and I can refer to my list throughout my day and week to make sure I am staying on point and reaching my goals.

Every Sunday, between noon and five, I reach for my white legal pad and begin to make my list of things I want to accomplish during the coming week. I never go to two pages even if I have to write very small. I use one page with two alligator clips at the bottom to hold it together throughout the abuse of the week. At the top of the page, I always write, "I prosper as I live a life of purpose," and, "To whom much is given, much is demanded," to remind myself that everything I do is for a bigger reason. I always begin with a clean sheet of paper, so each week starts off fresh. Sometimes the list has items from the previous week that didn't get done. I have found that because I am a habitual multitasker, this handwritten list keeps me on track for accomplishing my goals. I try not to overcommit each day because I want to get done what is on my list. I also believe in self-imposed deadlines on my lists. A goal without a deadline is only a dream.

As I write my weekly/daily to-do list, I also write a short "don't do" list. This list usually contains a few items that tend to keep me from accomplishing my goals each week. Don't dos are things like 1) stop wasting time by listening to office gossip, 2) stop letting associates use me as their shrink, or 3) stop going to meetings without an agenda.

I like to place "don't do" key words on a yellow sticky and stick it on my laptop screen edge. In the above case, my note would say "gossip, shrink, agenda." I hate spending energy and valuable time on mindless activities because after they're over, I look back and wish I had those thirty-nine minutes back in my life.

I divide the page into equal blocks. I write the days of the week in five blocks (Monday–Friday), and then I add a general block. I get out my old-school paper calendar (not a digital calendar) and see what I have scheduled for that week. From there, I start filling in my daily goals. I write everything on this one piece of paper, from "negotiate terms to sell X company" to "get my teeth cleaned." This routine really keeps me laser-focused. In addition to my weekly to-do list, I keep a long-term, handwritten list of goals that I refer to as my Get It Done List. This collection of thoughts is made up of things I want to stay focused on in the long term, things I do not want to forget. These items include everything from selling a company to planning unique travels to funding a philanthropic venture. I rewrite this list every Sunday as a way of reminding myself of what still needs to get done. I am a project-oriented person who needs to see that there is an end to a process. This handwritten list provides clarity on what it will take to get there.

The other benefit of creating a handwritten to-do list is that it makes you accountable, even if it's only to yourself. It's important to keep track of where you are and how far you've come. Handwritten lists are an excellent way to monitor your progress on a yearly, monthly, weekly, and daily basis.

ORTHODOX PATH: Type your weekly and annual goals in an Excel spreadsheet.

SPARKS PATH: Handwrite your weekly and annual goals on paper, as powerful things take place between the fingertips and the brain. Cross off your to-do list each time you complete a task—it will amaze you how good it feels each time you do it! The sense of accomplishment is incredible and will propel you to do more.

Meetings Don't Have to Suck

A special shout out to my friend Mark Henson of Sparkspace, who helped me find the words to articulate this next bit of wisdom. Having sat in thousands of meetings, I am somewhat of an expert as to how to conduct productive meetings and eliminate large wastes of time. Here are a few of my tried-and-true tips for conducting a quality meeting:

Know Your Purpose: Identify the purpose of your meeting. There are dozens of legit reasons to call a meeting, such as project status reports, brainstorming, or strategic planning. The key to a successful meeting is to pick one reason you are having the meeting and focus on that one reason. The biggest mistake most people make is trying to cover too much ground in a single meeting. I'd rather have three focused, productive meetings than a typical unfocused, schizophrenic meeting.

Publish Your Purpose: Send the agenda out ahead of time so people know what to expect in the meeting. People love to be able to think about the meat of the meeting, and this gives them a heads-up so they can prepare instead of trying to respond within seconds of learning the topic of the meeting.

Meet Like There Is No Tomorrow: If you knew the world were ending tomorrow and you had to have a meeting today, you wouldn't waste any time, would you? You'd watch both the agenda and the time. Unless you're having a free-flowing, blue-sky brainstorming session, most meetings should be short and sweet and always—always—start and end on time.

Be an Action Hero: A meeting without action is _____.

What word(s) did you use to fill in the blank? Boring? Typical? Frustrating? A waste of time? Every meeting should end with a review of action items. The best approach is to write down the action items as the meeting progresses, and to record the deadline and the name of the primary person responsible for each action item.

Repeat Yourself: One person in the meeting must be held accountable to document those action items, responsible parties, and deadlines. Send an email summary of action items to everyone who attended the meeting.

Delegate Responsibilities: Once you've set the action steps, delegate the responsibility of completing each specific item to someone you can hold accountable. Having a plan and a deadline for every deliverable will ensure each person understands his or her role in completing the task. Having a to-do list with deliverable dates is crucial to the success of any project. If everyone is following the same list, everyone is moving in the same direction.

Set a Due Date and Time for Each Deliverable: Remember, a goal without a deadline is only a dream! I am really big on setting unusual times and dates for deliverables because it gets the attention of the people involved. For example, I might ask to see the finished brochure on Friday at 10:42 a.m. These odd times create a sense of urgency that just isn't there when you say a standard time, such as Friday by 5 p.m. In fate, "Friday at 5 p.m." implies "Monday is fine, too." My tactic may seem unusual, but believe me, it is highly effective. For six years, we conducted a three-day event in Dallas for several thousand of our Wizetrade customers. We always listed odd times in the agenda for when sessions would begin or end (e.g., "Breakout Session X starts at 10:32"). This always generated an insane amount of buzz! I remember people coming up to our management team saying, "This is so cool . . . what's up with the strange times?" Obviously, we did this to create an impression, but we also did it to create a sense of "Got to be there at 10:32 or it will start without me."

Conversely, you don't want to say you're going to deliver something on a certain date or at a specific time and then fail to do it. When you don't follow through, you inadvertently send a message that failing to deliver on time is acceptable. If you say you're going to do something, then you have to do it or pay the price for missing the deadline.

If you're not early, you are late. Period. To help avoid being late, set your watch and clocks ten minutes ahead—at a minimum. This act makes you think about time.

Admittedly, I am an over-observant, multitasking, habitual, and somewhat cynical person. I firmly believe that performance is everything, and doing what you say you are going to do matters most. It may sound simple, but most people don't get it. Sooner or later, you are going to have to step up and perform. Think of that tight performance schedule as a winner's challenge and an opportunity to shine.

Daily Dashboards

When most people get into their cars, the first thing they do after turning on the ignition is take a look at the dashboard. Why? The dashboard provides the crucial information you need to know to be sure everything is safe and secure. If there's a problem, a light comes on to warn you that something needs your attention. You can then gauge whether it's an immediate concern or one that can wait a day or even a week or more to address.

In business, a dashboard report visually presents crucial data in summary form so you can make quick and effective decisions about when and how to deal with each item. I use a daily dashboard to summarize the crucial facts of my dealings for that day, month, and year to date. I've created daily dashboards and received them from staff members of every business I have ever been associated with for the past thirty-five years. They're a great way to get a real read on the business. I like to get my dashboards, like clockwork, by 8:33 each morning. Dashboards don't have to come from some fancy software that gathers the critical data points for you. A dashboard can be a gathering of data points that someone in your office researches from various associates each morning and assembles into one spot for the management team to review.

Every dashboard is a little different because it relates to your specific business. In general, a dashboard might look something like this:

Cash on Hand:	**$145,412**
Receivables:	**$212,109**
Accrued Payables to Date:	**$112,587**
Total Customers Sold Yesterday:	24
Total Customers Sold Month to Date:	179
Total Customers Paying Monthly:	19,256
Total Customers Canceled YTD:	140
Average Monthly Payment Received:	$149
Total Staff Employed:	74
Total Staff Contracted:	3
Total Office Rent per Month:	$5,689

If you and your management team see this information each day, you will clearly have a handle on where you were, where you are, and where you are going. That, in turn, will give you a tremendous sense of confidence to successfully run the day-to-day and future operations of your business.

ORTHODOX PATH: Maintain critical business data in separate places, and distribute it only when absolutely necessary.

SPARKS PATH: Maintain a daily dashboard of critical data, and share it with the management team by 8:33 each morning.

Validation and Recognition = Motivation

When Barack Obama became president, America was full of optimism that this new guy, whom most people had never heard of before the election, would bring change to our country. Actually, President Obama gave us the idea of hope more than the promise of change. Hope is a powerful thing—it invokes confidence, courage, promise, excitement, anticipation, expectation, optimism, and faith. Some pretty impressive thoughts make up the idea of hope. Hope is also infectious.

When it comes to business, the same principles apply. In fact, I use the promise of hope every day. I make statements such as, "I am really hopeful we will launch this product by Friday at 2:12." What I am really saying is that even though I know we are challenged, I believe someday in the near future, we will succeed. I am also expressing my confidence in the people I've selected to perform the tasks, letting them know I think they are the right people for this project and I know they'll perform well.

I don't like to lead with negative words, so I do my best to frame items of concern in a positive manner. This approach inspires people to try harder instead of shutting them down with disappointment. When an associate comes into my office and says, "I would like to take on more responsibility," what he is really saying is that he wants a raise. What I try to figure out is why I should give him one. I always listen and might respond with something like, "I am hopeful you will get there, too. In fact, even though you aren't quite there yet, you should be excited about the prospect, because if you keep doing the time and grinding away, you will get there." By offering him this type of support and hope, I am fanning the flame instead of dousing it with water. Keeping associates excited by the possibilities (offering them hope) is one of the best ways to keep them motivated and rowing in the same direction. I realize the idea sounds simple, but don't underestimate its power!

While money is a great motivator, it isn't always the most powerful or effective way to earn loyalty from your team. There's great danger in offering annual bonuses because I have found that most associates simply assume it will happen every year. When you give a bonus once a year, you automatically set the precedent and expectation that the money isn't based on performance as much as it's based on obligation. Realistically speaking, businesses can have excess revenues one year and none the next. Not being able to pay an annual bonus under such circumstances can be a catastrophically demotivating event.

I have found that doing something proactive, such as running a contest where first prize is not cash but a tangible item such as a sixty-inch flat-screen television, is much more beneficial. I like to display the award in the office for a couple of weeks to get the staff talking. It's human nature to like receiving trophies because it's a form of validation for being the best at something. On the last episode of her talk show, Oprah Winfrey said that after twenty-five years of interviews, the one thing all of her guests had in common was the need to be validated. Recognition is an inherent need in all of us. Awards are badges of honor; they are acknowledgements before your peers that you did something better than everyone else did. A popular statement these days around our Splash Media office is, "You're a rock star." It's meant as a compliment when someone does something really good. We zeroed in on that expression and made a "Rock Star" trophy by filling an empty can of Rock Star energy drink with enough plaster to give it weight. Then we affixed a one-inch acrylic base to it with the Splash Media logo and the words, "You Are a Rock Star," engraved on it. The winner each week is determined by a peer vote, and the recipient is always announced with lots of fanfare, cheers, and handshakes.

The problem with most bonus programs is that as soon as the terms are released, a significant portion of the *sales* team knows they can't win, so they are more discouraged than encouraged to produce. It's far better to customize bonuses based on individual goals and then reward only those who have met their goals. This ensures that everybody has a chance to win, and everyone remains motivated. It's imperative to recognize and reward success—in fact, rewarding success is contagious.

ORTHODOX PATH: Bring an associate in your office and pat him or her on the back for doing a fine job.

SPARKS PATH: Publicly praise an associate in an all-staff meeting and recognize him or her with a small token (not monetary) of your appreciation.

The A-Team

Another tool I've used is the creation of an A-Team. There are approximately forty-five or so people throughout my career who have received a customized American gold coin ring that signifies they are lifers to me, which means they are a part of my inner sanctum. We also add their names to the list of the other A-Teamers on a plaque that reads:

"An A-Teamer is an individual who sees a challenge and resolves it without the need for acknowledgement, understands the vision of the company and takes ownership of it, is dedicated and loyal to the success of the company for a lifetime, is motivated by the love of his or her work rather than by money, has earned respect and admiration of coworkers, and always seeks more responsibility."

These people will always be a big part of how and why I've been able to reach the level of success I have. In a way, it's as if we are all members of the same tribe or fraternity, and we're all committed and loyal to the same goal. I know that every single person who wears an A-Team ring has my back. They all know I have theirs as well. Every individual who has received A-Team status sheds a tear or two at the time of receipt. I most enjoy awarding this status in front of the entire staff. Peer-to-peer recognition is more powerful than words can express.

When my longtime assistant Trish first interviewed to work with me, she immediately noticed the A-Team rings a few people in the office were wearing. She asked about the significance of them during our interview. When I told her what it meant to me, she responded, "I am going to get one of those rings someday."

"We'll see," I said. I admired her tenacity from the start, so I hired her on the spot. From that day forward, whenever she'd do something I thought was excellent, I'd send her a little note with a smiley face that simply read, "Great Job!" or "All Good!"

Inevitably, Trish would come to me and say, "I know it was great, but was it A-Team worthy?"

Trish eventually received her ring, right around the time we closed the acquisition of a large auto insurance agency. I called her into my office to give her a bonus check as a token of my appreciation for all she had done to help close that purchase. Next to her envelope was a ring box. Trish's eyes lit up like a Christmas tree—at the sight of the box, not the check. She was over the moon to finally have a ring and cried like a baby with tears of joy.

There is a time, however, when money does talk louder than anything else—and that's when you have the distinct honor and privilege of sharing the wealth after a liquidity event (sale of a company). When I sold GlobalTec Solutions, there were seventeen people from our organization who received life-changing bonuses they never knew were coming. They proved their worth and relevance each and every day we built that company, even on the very day we closed the sale to another organization. There was no promise they would benefit from their hard work—but there was always hope.

After the sale closed, I gave those seventeen people less than twenty-four hours' notice of a private, invitation-only dinner at the Mercury Grill in Dallas. Naturally, everyone showed up, and when they got to the table, there was an envelope tied in a red bow at each place setting. I didn't let them open their envelopes until they got to their cars after dinner. There were two things inside the envelopes: a check that ranged from hundreds of thousands to millions of dollars, and very specific instructions on how to be a good steward with the money. The letter explained that the money they just received was going to be heavily taxed by Uncle Sam, so they needed to know up front that they must first pay the 35 percent ordinary income tax. Second, if they had the opportunity to pay off their house, my suggestion was to use the enclosed money to do just that. I have always strongly believed in living a debt-free life, including, if possible, living in a home that is completely paid for. It might become your greatest asset someday and could be used to fall back on in times of need. Not having the burden of a house payment hanging over your head each month is powerful and liberating. It is amazing how confident one becomes when he or she has no debt. My hope was to inspire these seventeen people to do the same and not live beyond their means. Several of the people there that night considered permanent retirement, but most were far too young to last in that mindset for long.

I had justly rewarded everyone who had worked his or her hardest to help build GlobalTec Solutions. I wanted to take care of them as they had taken care of the business and me. Most of these people weren't going to stay at the company under the new ownership, so I thought it was a great way for everyone to go out. I call this tact "spread it and let it go." Allocating these bonuses gave me the best feeling in the world. Sharing the profit was far better than actually selling the company—which was an incredible high for all of us. I fondly look back on that night, knowing I did the right thing.

I remember hearing a speech given by General Norman Schwarzkopf regarding his 14 Rules of Leadership. I've never forgotten his fourteenth rule, which is simply, "do the right thing." It is a sign of character. Character requires a sense of ethics, duty, and morality, and if you've lived your life with these characteristics, you will effectively lead others through your own example. With such strength of character, you will always make the right decision and have the courage to stand tall in that decision. Deep down, we all know the right thing to do. Audacity to follow through is the line that separates a great leader from all others. That's why giving the unexpected, life-changing bonuses to everyone that night was such an easy decision for me.

It truly is far better to give than receive. Although . . .

Just as we were leaving that night, there was a rather big surprise waiting for me—one I had no idea was coming, which made it even better. Greg Schardt, a partner and lead GlobalTec software engineer, presented me with a pristine, completely refurbished, classic 1957 Corvette convertible. Seeing it in the parking lot was like being in a dream. The car had a black exterior with a gray scoop on the side and a candy-apple red leather interior. When I received the car, it only had fifty-seven miles on it. Today there are only three hundred twenty-four miles on its fully restored engine. The vintage classic is pure muscle and was the fifty-seventh Corvette to come off of the assembly line in 1957, not coincidentally the year I was born.

I wasn't expecting anything, especially because I was doing the giving that night. When Greg handed me the keys, I felt like a kid who'd just received his driver's license and his first new car. I was overwhelmed with appreciation, and for once in my life, I was truly speechless. Still today, every time I fire her up, she reminds me of that wonderful evening when my peers extended such a remarkable display of gratitude, and I am also reminded about the many times we were in the trenches together and came out victorious.

Another unexpected surprise was the two-week, first-class, all-expenses-paid trip to Italy that my assistant Trish presented to my wife and me as a token of her appreciation. I'm talking the presidential suite at the most famous hotel on Lake Como,

Italy. That kind of first class! It blew my mind because I am a guy who enjoys taking care of others. Learning to become a gracious receiver was a hard lesson for me, but I also understood the thrill and fulfillment one experiences when giving from his or her heart. There was nothing more important to me than allowing my trusted colleagues the same satisfaction I feel every time I share the wealth. Yes, sometimes it is better to give than to receive, and other times it's really nice to just sit back and accept the selfless kindness of others.

ORTHODOX PATH: Retain the wealth entirely for the owner of the company.

SPARKS PATH: "Rule 14 – Do the Right Thing." Share the success and wealth with the team that helped you get the brass ring in the first place.

Act Fast

Have you ever tried to talk about or make a speech about a subject you didn't believe in? Chances are, without that important connection, your presentation ended up being really lousy. For me, if I don't believe in something, I get out of it—and fast. However, if I do believe, I can make miracles happen in Sparks Speed time.

After starting Splash Media, I was looking to acquire a company that would help bring an additional social media component (the secret sauce) to our infrastructure. Chris Kraft told me about a Dallas-based Internet consulting business called WebDex. The company was owned by Paul Slack, who had the foresight to start an Internet marketing business in 1999, prior to the birth of social media and long before it became mainstream for companies to have websites. WebDex was one of the first companies in the Dallas area to effectively use the Internet to market directly to its clients.

The purpose of Paul's company was to help business-to-business companies leverage the Internet. They were working on a retained business model where they received flat fees every month to deliver value to their customers exclusively through the web. Paul was able to effectively woo accounts with his ability to not only build a website for them, but also to handle all of their web marketing needs, from email blasts to customer service. Within WebDex's first year in business, the company had grown to ten employees and was servicing fifty accounts—a respectable number given the size of the operation.

By the time we met, Paul had been in business for ten years, and the only problem I could identify with WebDex was that they hadn't grown any bigger than they were after that first year in business. In short, Paul didn't know how to take his company to the next level. By default, he had become their limiting factor because he had his hand in every pot. Although his primary responsibility was running the company, he was also like a super account manager. He could effectively develop strategies for his clients, but ironically not for his own company. This is a classic mistake entrepreneurs frequently make—one that prevents them from breaking through their own self-imposed barriers to success.

But Chris Kraft was unrelenting in his belief that our two companies needed to work together. The idea made a lot of sense because we had the funding and the highest-quality production facility in Dallas, and Paul had the managing service model. Together we could effectively exploit our various products. To make the introduction, Chris suggested that we take Paul to lunch and discuss the ways we could come together in business.

Despite my general aversion to "doing lunch," there have been a couple of unavoidable occasions when I've reluctantly said yes, but you can bet I always empty my pockets before I go. I really don't like going to lunch with people, as most have an agenda and are ready to attack. Once you're at the table, they think they've got you cornered—and they do. You're stuck as a captive audience whether or not you're interested. I have walked away from many lunches and thought, "I can't believe I put myself in a position to let this person corner me." There were much better ways to spend those hours, and I almost always regretted my decisions to go. One thing I am certain of is that I will never have lunch with bankers, insurance agents, or brokers of any kind ever again because, without fail, those meetings end up being a colossal waste of my time.

So, having lunch with Paul Slack was a rare occasion—not because I went, but because it turned out to be worth it. I sat with Chris, Paul, and Mark Hitchner, listening as each spoke. I often ask a few questions and then listen. If you wait long enough, everything you want to know will eventually come out. I liked what I was hearing because I suddenly felt my right knee begin to bounce! We were in the midst of creating the outsourcing social media company of the decade, and that was very exciting.

Even though Paul insisted his company wasn't for sale, he quickly got on board with the vision we had at Splash Media. It was a match made in heaven. Within a month of that lunch meeting, I acquired WebDex. Paul moved his entire operation to our campus, and the rest is history.

The Splash Media team and I were confident from the start that Paul and his team had much to add to what we were already doing, but that didn't necessarily make it easy for Paul to acclimate to some of my unorthodox ways. He came in hoping to help us become more process-oriented and better organized. I, however, didn't have any interest in that approach. Getting mired down in hypotheticals that look good on paper but are meaningless once a project is up and running can lead to a condition I call *analysis paralysis*. While Paul was very big on workflows, business plans, and organizational charts, I think those things are generally a waste of time and energy. Naturally, he thought I was crazy for my run-and-gun, let's-not-overthink-it approach to business. After all, he had made a career of thinking critically about every decision—from hiring to firing and everything in between. Yet despite spending ten years trying to plot the future of his company using different methods to predict what would happen, deep down Paul knew better than anyone that such predictions never look the same as the future reality. Working with us, Paul soon began to realize that without organizational charts, you have no choice but to *work* your business. When you do, the stars always rise. You can spot the weaknesses that hold your product or service back and correct those weaknesses instantly. He discovered that it is far more exciting and effective to analyze something in real time and under real conditions than under hypothetical ones.

Paul had worked in high gear for ten years at WebDex, always putting in long days and endless hours of his time, but when we joined forces, he was exposed to a whole new speed—Sparks Speed—a pace I'm pretty sure he never knew existed. Sparks Speed isn't something that's found in most people's gearboxes. It's true that the speed I am most comfortable working at can be grueling for others, but it can also be very exciting. I am always on fast-forward, and that way of operating can really help change the thinking of associates who have done business differently in the past. When I tell someone to go I don't mean, "Go think, go analyze, and go plan." I mean, "Go, go, and do!"

Another new concept for Paul and his team was working in an environment where there were no job titles. I explained to him that without specific definitions, you actually create an environment in which people feel they have the ability and freedom to do *everything* instead of just one thing. It's a great approach, ensuring that all bases are always covered because everyone who works at the company has each other's back. There's no separation as to whose job it is to get something done because we are all working toward the same goal, juggling however many balls it takes to get that job done in a scrappy entrepreneurial environment. I call this my "everyone sweeps the floor" theory. I work hard and smart, and I expect everyone around me to do the same. I want to set the example, tone, and pace that will help us win the race. There is no job beneath me, and if I am willing to do it, my team members should be willing to as well. If they're not, they will never last in business—at least not with me.

ORTHODOX PATH: Everyone gets a job title. Reporting structures are set in stone, and you report only to your superior.

SPARKS PATH: Titles for no one! Everyone earns the respect of each associate on his or her own merits. Associates learn to work with each other and for each other. Amazing things happen when associates feel accountable to each other instead of to a single boss.

Listen to Your Gut

Gut instinct plays a huge part in everything you do as a leader. Leadership is an art, not a science. You have to learn to listen to your gut and then do what it tells you.

Learning to listen to your gut comes with living life and having experiences along the way. So much of business is based on gut feelings, yet most people ignore them. Acting on your instincts means you have total conviction about what you believe to be true, and you have the courage to do something about that conviction. Some of this could be seen as risk taking, but it isn't foolish risk taking. When I get a gut feeling, I just know that what I'm doing is right. I can feel the synchronicity in every fiber of my being. Most of the time, I am dead on, and I end up wondering why no one else can see what I am seeing. When I explain to the team why I believe everything is perfectly aligned, I automatically assume they can see it as well. More often than not, they get it; but if they don't, it won't stop me from taking action. I have the confidence, courage, and belief in myself to push through anyway.

To move through the world effectively, you've got to have your priorities established. You've got to know what you believe in and be willing to stand firm in those beliefs. You need confidence in yourself and in the experiences that have led you here. You get nothing for nothing. Creating a business and keeping it afloat is hard work.

You also have to be willing to pull the trigger to make the tough decisions. Nothing is more debilitating to an organization than a leader who won't make a decision of any kind. The whole organization just stops and waits and nothing happens because a leader won't make a choice. That hesitation and lack of commitment will paralyze an organization. When you are in command, you have to take charge. If you don't, someone else will, usually an outside company or someone from within who may be planning a coup.

My style of business can be very polarizing. People either have what it takes to adapt or they quit. There is no gray area. If Paul Slack were to survive in our world, he had little choice but to take nearly half of everything he knew about business and let it go. He had read dozens of management and sales books, but now he had to place his trust in someone he barely knew and in a new style of working that went against the grain of everything he had practiced before. But Paul is a very smart guy who saw where we were headed. Once he realized that we didn't bring him in to change our machine, that we had acquired his company so we could apply the things he was really good at, he jumped aboard our speeding bullet train and took the journey with us. When he was finally able to get over the mental hurdle of doing things in a whole new and still uncomfortable way, he truly committed himself. He was all in.

If you are smart and confident and you see an opportunity, you have to pounce on it like a chicken on a june bug. You have to take the risk to seize that chance because great possibilities don't come around every day. Don't overthink it. Just do it! You don't have to sit back and ponder every detail of where you want to go before pulling the trigger. Just do it! It's completely okay to learn along the way. In fact, experience is the best teacher. It's like flying an airplane at 30,000 feet while building it. It can be done as long as you have the basics in place.

Sometimes when times get tough, I simply stand up and walk away for a few hours to get some clarity on the challenge I'm facing. Ninety-nine percent of the time, I return with an idea to take one more step forward. I'll get in my car and just drive to a bookstore or a mall and just walk. You must dig deep within your soul to find a way to succeed if you truly have a great product; however, be ready to dodge and weave because what you start with today will most likely not be what you sell tomorrow.

ORTHODOX PATH: Make every decision by committee and publicly hang those who make mistakes.

SPARKS PATH: Let leaders make decisions and mistakes without fear. Embrace failure as learning something you won't do again. Fail fast and fix faster!

B.A.M.—Believe, Achieve, and Master

This section provides a step-by-step breakdown of the things you will need to consider when setting out to build your own successful company. Remember, these insights come from years of "Sparks Speed" experience, trial and error, failure and success. I always tell people that true success is found by identifying your passion and seizing the opportunity. Success is not found in the job—it is found in the passion. Set your sights on the dreams you want to attain, and then have the courage to Believe, Achieve, and Master (a practice I call B.A.M.). Success is not the key to success; the journey to success is the key to success. If you love what you are doing, you will be successful.

This is why it is so important to *believe* in what you're doing 100 percent. Rest assured that if you don't, no one else will.

Next, continuously strive to *achieve* as you reach each goal you've set along the way.

And finally, *master* whatever it is you are doing.

The principles behind B.A.M. sound easy enough to follow, but they're not. They're extremely hard. Say, for example, you are passionate about cooking, art, cars, social networking, software, or health care. You must be realistic. You might not have what it takes to become the next Steven Spielberg, but you can find your calling by staying within your passion sphere. Become an assistant director, hone your skills, and learn the trade so you can use your passion to fulfill your dream. Both passion and tenacity have to be there, because building a successful business is fraught with challenges. Creating and then operating a business is like running a marathon. It's a nonstop pursuit of survival, and if you're focused and prepared to weave and dodge, success is inevitable.

If you're already in business, take the time to read the details in this section and assess the elements you are currently implementing. More important, identify those you aren't using. If you are just starting a new company, read this section of the book and implement each of these elements to help you get and stay on the right path.

Believe, Achieve, and Master. B.A.M.!

Learn to say "no." I explained my reasons for saying "no" to lunch dates and how doing so allows me to gain at least five hours a week, but there are lots of other, everyday sneaky distractions you should learn to say "no" to as well.

"No" is a complete sentence, and saying it will help you prune distractions from your life and allow you to focus on what is truly important.

Faith, Passion, Tenacity

In our offices, we have these words emblazoned on our walls:

"Faith, Passion, Tenacity, Focus, Monetization, and an Outrageous Sense of Urgency"

The words are self-explanatory, but each possesses a powerful meaning to our entire staff and the guests who often ask about them.

- **Faith.** In my opinion, one should try to find faith in a higher being. My faith has brought me through hell and back a few times in my life, and without a higher being to rely on, I might have simply put a bullet in my head. Far be it for me to suggest a particular religion; however, finding a powerful spiritual foundation has proven extremely valuable in my life and my business.

- **Passion.** Passion is desperately required in all facets of business. The difference between a passionate associate and one who is only working for a paycheck is remarkable for the short- and long-term success of your business.

- **Tenacity.** All businesses today require a tremendous amount of gut-wrenching tenacity to succeed. A cupcake bakery isn't going to be successful if it isn't tenacious in quality, marketing, and beating the competition.

- **Monetization.** Keeping a very sharp eye on monetizing each facet of your business is critical to your success. We often get caught up in the muck of running a business, but at the end of the day, it's all about dollars.

- **Outrageous Sense of Urgency.** Maintaining an ultrafast-paced environment in your office creates infectious enthusiasm and a momentum that everyone wants to be a part of. Life and business bring us all kinds of daily obstacles. Getting done today what you could have done tomorrow relieves a tremendous amount of pressure.

I urge every business owner to find words of sincere meaning and post them in public for your associates' and customers' reflection. Consider asking some team members to help you decide what three words you are most proud of . . . words you would love to explain to every new associate and customer who walks in your door.

Correctly Name Your Company and Product

Naming your company should be an exhausting endeavor; it requires your putting in a ton of effort to avoid screwing up this critical element. Many entrepreneurs make the mistake of thinking they ought to name their companies after themselves. Although there are several examples of brands that have done well under this premise, there are countless others that haven't fared nearly as well. It's a gamble for a new company, especially when there is no platform or brand already established to explain what the product is or exactly what the company does.

Consider, for example, a company like Dell Computers. Michael Dell used his name as a banner for the company. This branding tactic is extremely dangerous. Luckily for Michael Dell, it worked, but only because Dell produced a great product at a great time and invested hundreds of millions of dollars in advertising (branding). There was one point in time, however, when Michael had stepped away from running the day-to-day business, was no longer on the board of directors, and was semiretired. Imagine what would have happened if the company had tanked in his absence. Both he and Dell Computers would have been equally tagged as failures for the rest of Michael's—and his company's—life. The best and most current example of such taint can clearly be seen in the case of the Madoffs. Bernard L. Madoff Investment Securities, LLC was named after its founder, Bernie Madoff, the convicted felon and admitted operator of a Ponzi scheme that is considered the largest financial fraud in U.S. history. Would you ever do business with anyone associated with Madoff, his investment firm, or even his family? The name is synonymous with fraud, deceit, and scams.

Another reason I don't recommend using your name is that it lowers the value of the company should you decide to sell. What good are 200 locations of Marc Sparks Donut Shops without Marc Sparks? While I know of only a few companies that have bought a name for marquee value, most want the man (or woman) behind the brand if you name your company after yourself. I'm not saying don't do it, but you can bet there is a 95 percent chance that naming a business with your name attached to it will come back to haunt you in some way.

Another common mistake that inexperienced entrepreneurs make early in the game is trying to get too cute with the names of their products or company. The name of your company should reflect the image you want to project to the world. Honey Bunny Hat Shop just sounds ridiculous. If ridiculous is what you're aiming for, then go for it. But if you're like most entrepreneurs, you will probably want to be taken seriously for the work you do and for the products you make.

Selecting the name of your company may seem like an easy process, but it's not. Be prepared for a real roller-coaster ride in picking a name today. You can come up with the perfect name, but once you start doing a little research, you might find that someone else's business already has that name . . . and the web domain, too. You can pick a hundred different names, and if you're lucky, maybe one or two will be available. For example, when we started a rehabilitation hospital company, I liked the name Reliant. The word "reliant" portrays confidence and strength to me. We conducted a search and found that there are hundreds of Reliant organizations out there, but none were a rehabilitation hospital. Initially, you can search without hiring an attorney. Simply go online and type in the domain you would be using to see if it is has been taken. In my case, I typed in www.reliantrehabilitationhospital.com, and to my surprise, it was a go! I immediately purchased the domain name and everything around it. I bought the .net, .com, .org, and a dozen odd configurations of the name, too. Next, I contacted our attorney and asked him to reserve the name in Texas so we could incorporate and expand nationally from there. I did all of this while my wonderful graphic arts magician, Megan Sullivan, was developing our logo.

Most entrepreneurs have a space outside their office for their personal assistants, but I like to have my webmaster/graphic designer there instead. Megan has worked with me (not for me— get it?) for more than fifteen years and has occupied a nearby desk ever since I can remember. She is the first person I call out to when I get an idea that I need to bring to life visually. We communicate with each other as though we are using our own particular brand of shorthand. I say a few things that wouldn't make a lot of sense to most other people, but is somehow perfectly clear to her. What a gem! In typical Sparks Speed fashion, we had a name and logo within an hour.

ORTHODOX PATH: Show little regard
to naming your business by egotistically
using your given name in the title.

SP

SPARKS PATH: Pay an outrageous amount
of attention to naming your business.
Don't be single-minded; make sure you
give the business a BIG name that can be
seen as more than a one-trick pony.

A few months later, someone with whom I worked closely while building Reliant Rehabilitation Hospitals approached me to develop a similar project. He had enough experience to get the project off the ground, and, if he could stay focused, he surely would have been the guy to do it. There was just one problem. I hated (I don't use "hate" often) the name he had chosen for his new venture, and it was nearing a point of no return. Plus, I didn't think he had the right direction or focused passion. He was all over the place, trying to be everything to everybody. I coached him and told him to call me when he found some clarity on the project. As badly as I wanted to do the project with him, I had to pass at that point in time.

Reliant Healthcare Partners was another grand slam! We built a half-dozen hospitals, had a few more on the drawing board (valuable momentum), employed more than a 1,000 associates, and sold the company four years later for a very respectable multimillion-dollar figure. The project was a winner from the start, thanks mainly to the passion and tenacity of my cofounder and partner, Emmitt Moore.

Still, after hearing about his idea, and in anticipation of moving forward on my own, I formed a new company called Cobalt Medical Partners. I thought the name represented a strong, bold brand. I was actually stunned that the name and the domain were both available, so we grabbed them while we could. Powerful names are pure gold. Over the years, I have amassed a library of domain names so I can easily choose from them when naming a new company or venture and know that they will be available. Other powerful names I have used in my startups include the following (among many others):

- U.S. Fidelity Holding Corporation
- Unistar
- Consolidated Surety Agency
- Great Southern General Agency
- First Choice
- The Hinsdale Collection
- Peppers Bar and Grill

- Reliant Healthcare Partners
- Eagle Premium Finance Company
- Consolidated Risk Management Company
- First United Investment Company
- Splash Media, LP
- Splash Media University
- SplashCube
- BlueJay Wireless
- Cardinal Wireless Distributors
- Link Wireless Distributors
- GlobalTec Solutions
- Wizetrade
- Options Made Easy
- Forex Made Easy
- CommandTRADE
- InsureTec Solutions
- Total Med Solutions
- Cobalt Medical Partners
- Timber Creek Capital
- Cobalt Real Estate Services

As I suspected, a few months later, the young man came back to me and said he was ready to share his focused strategy. He had clearly fine-tuned his vision and had found another capital partner to back him. When I looked at the financial arrangements he had made with the other partner, the final outcome didn't suit me, so I reluctantly passed again. I ended up giving him the Cobalt Medical Partners Texas state corporation designation, domain name, and logo design, and wished him tremendous success. He took my gift and is thriving today!

No Partners

Other than passionate founders, I have made it a point over the years to avoid taking on partners. Simply stated, working with partners is like having too many cooks in the kitchen. I rather enjoy being the primary decision maker, particularly when it's my time and money at stake. I have been baptized by fire, and the thought of having to explain the method to my madness all day long is exhausting. Partners are especially cumbersome to an entrepreneur like me because they usually approach business from a purely monetary and orthodox standpoint, which is the complete opposite direction of where I come from. I don't do boards either. The few boards I've sat on always remind me of exactly why I don't like being on them. Entrepreneurs and people of vision need thought leaders to bounce ideas off. The last thing we need is people who are dedicated to holding us down. I have often said that the giraffe must have been designed by a committee.

Other than rare exceptions, the only time I deviate from my no-partners rule is when the person is or has been an entrepreneur or when we need the person for long-term, strategic reasons. If I take on a new project, I will offer the entrepreneur a percentage of the company while I retain the majority share. I keep the bigger piece because I am the financial partner who has money at risk, and I am usually the day-to-day operations partner until the business gets on its feet. Nearly every project I take on is not bankable. The risk of loss to a traditional financial institution is too great, and they want nothing to do with these types of projects. One of my secret weapons is that I also provide the infrastructure for each business, including the growth capital, legal advice, accounting, IT, HR, office space, marketing, graphics, packaging, staffing, mentoring, and anything else the business needs to get off the ground. I am usually the one burdened with all of the issues that can and do arise. I am careful not to dilute the partner's percentage, as I want him or her to come on board fully, staying focused on the essence of the business, not the day-to-day minutiae that derail most entrepreneurs.

If you absolutely must take a partner, never do a 50/50 partnership. Even if the partner is a family member, a 50/50 split is a really bad idea. In all partnerships, one partner really does have the leg up on the other partner in one way or another, and a 51/49 partnership sets the tone and sends a message: "If we ever come to push and shove, I trust you will do the right thing." This is true for founders, too. I have often looked at founders of companies I have invested in and said, "Bob, we have debated this to death. You are the founder, and this is your baby—you have to make the final decision." Someone has to be the one who makes the final decision in all matters, and you might as well set that process up for success in the beginning.

ORTHODOX PATH: Take on partners and shareholders to spread the risk.

SPARKS PATH: Rarely take on partners or shareholders, as they usually end up becoming a tremendous distraction, and the lost opportunity cost is much greater than their contribution.

Business Plans Are for Goobers

As you read earlier, after I lost my megabusiness, Unistar, I placed a simple 6" x 3" tombstone ad in the Dallas newspaper looking for business ventures. I intentionally asked for a simple business summary in lieu of a business plan. I have a long-standing belief that business plans are for the very naïve or—as I like to call them—goobers. Business schools teach the importance of writing a thorough business plan, but they don't tell their students that those plans are really just a bunch of crap. Most people don't realize that the day they launch a business, that plan is suddenly and swiftly obsolete. It breaks my heart to see so many people go through a grueling six-month (or longer) process, writing a half-inch-thick business plan for a start-up. None of it matters. It's wasted paper, and worse, wasted time that was spent over-planning instead of doing.

Creating a business plan requires the kind of overthinking that keeps you stuck in one place. It's the analysis paralysis I discussed earlier. Business plans are nothing more than a false sense of having to do business in an old-fashioned way. Business plans are best used as a sales tool to raise capital. Yes, it's the first thing many conservative venture capitalists, bankers, and angel investors usually ask for, although I cannot understand their reasons for wanting an overcomplicated bunch of baloney. Business plans are the last thing I want to see—ever. If you are talking to the right group of investors who can visualize what you are selling, you can literally throw everything else out because they will get on board if they like what they hear. Usually the ones asking for the materials are people who have never started a business in the first place, let alone run one successfully.

I am not suggesting that you don't do your homework; I am saying, however, that if you can't write your plan on one 8" x 11" sheet of paper with a financial forecast, you are not ready for prime time. For example, I love the popular television show *Shark Tank* because the panel of entrepreneurs and experts totally get it. An aspiring entrepreneur has a finite amount of time to explain her product and business model to four very successful entrepreneurs who have all made it big and have gone venture capitalist. These investors can either pass or bid on the proposed business right then and there. No business plan necessary! In less than five minutes, you either have it or you don't.

Everything I need to know about your company can be shared on a single piece of paper. If you can't accomplish that, you are obviously forcing a square peg into a round hole, and your business is destined to fail. That is why I asked for a business summary instead of a business plan in my ad.

1. A good one-page business summary includes the name of your product, a brief product description, the benefits to a buyer of your product, and the size of the market—something you should be able to convey in a few sentences without taking a breath. If you have to stop and explain your product, then it is too complicated and isn't something you can easily get to market. This is one area where you need to keep things simple.

2. Also, show me a prototype of the product. If you don't have one yet, what are the estimated costs of having one built?

3. Provide a one-line projection of revenue that simplifies the numbers for your investor. If you build your product for X and are planning on selling it for Y, your profit equals Z. Simple, easy to understand, and to the point— just the way I like it. There isn't an investor worth the check he writes who won't appreciate that kind of candor and straightforwardness.

4. I want to see something about your target market, too. How big is the universe you're trying to conquer? Everyone wants to claim his or her product is good for the masses, but in most cases, that's simply not true. The entire world neither wants nor needs your product, but if it's worthy, a portion of the population does. Tell

me about them. Be realistic and honest about your target market. It will help keep you focused on reaching them. For example:

- Is it for women ages 22-35?

- Men who are follicle-challenged?

- Families with young children?

5. Finally, how do you plan to reach your demographic? Will you use landing pages, TV commercials, long-form infomercials, short-form commercials, newspapers, seminars, associations, radio spots, billboards, magazines, trade shows, or social media? Will you launch a website? I am not looking for a marketing plan, but I would like to hear your thoughts about how to sell your product.

You may not think this limited information is enough data to lure an investor, but I know it is. I have invested in companies that have gone on to become very successful with just as few details. Of course, by now you know the story of George Thompson's software product, which was presented via fax and ultimately became Wizetrade and GlobalTec Solutions. The one line that read, "Give me five minutes of your time, and I will show you a stock-trading software tool that will change the world," was the only thing I needed to hear to take a very serious look at that business.

ORTHODOX PATH: Develop a thick business plan, and fill it full of financial models and projections. Spend months getting your plan just right.

SPARKS PATH: Develop a one-page executive summary in three hours or less.

First, Build the Box

OUTRAGEOUS or WOW "Packaging" is among the top five critical criteria needed to succeed in business.

Have you ever purchased a book because of its cover? Have you NOT purchased a book because it had an ugly or a blah cover? Thinking, "If the cover looks like that then what's inside must suck too."

Now, have you ever purchased a book because of its cover and years later you have yet to read it? Alas…we have all done it! We bought books because of the cover or packaging and never read them. I bet I have twenty books on my bookshelf that I have never read, but I know I purchased them simply because of the brilliant packaging.

One of my greatest secrets to successfully building a product or company is my God-given ability to instantly see the common sense in everything. So many people complicate things by getting too mired in microscopic details that simply do not matter. These are the same people who think that the more they talk, the smarter the world thinks they are. In reality, keeping your message concise and to the point is by far the best approach when it comes to business—especially when it comes to your product packaging.

My style has always been to first and foremost focus on packaging the product we are selling. This sounds counterintuitive as everyone likes to build the product first and then let that dictate the packaging and marketing. I found that building your packaging simultaneously with building your product—or even before you build the product—creates a canvas that allows you to develop a MUCH better product. We call it "designing the box first" strategy! Inevitably, if we start brainstorming on the packaging and text for the packaging it ultimately becomes the blueprint for the product we end up building.

For example, I may want to say on the packaging something like "as easy as red and green lights" in order to sell more product when I launch it. Well then I have to make sure the product inside the box will deliver an easy-to-use product! Once I can see the box or packaging, I can envision the product in 3-D. I've already built the box while everyone else is trying to figure out what to put inside the box. The contents are important, but not as important as the packaging. In a Sparks Speed world, the beautiful boxes will always be waiting for their content to arrive for distribution.

When I say packaging, I am talking about what it takes to display your product or service for market:

- Websites
- Landing Pages
- Logos
- Social Media Sites (Facebook, LinkedIn)
- Business Cards
- Letterhead
- Your Email Signature Line
- Collateral Material
- Labels and Boxes
- Book Covers

When George Thompson and I started Wizetrade, I actually designed the packaging before we had the finished software product to put into the box. My theory has always been that if you can't convey the idea of the product in the space of a napkin or sticky pad, you will never sell the product that goes inside the box. If you build the box first and then fill all of the panels around it, you are forced to look at every possible angle and talk about every feature and benefit of your product.

To me, a perfect package breaks down like this: on all of my collateral material, product features get 25 percent of the space, and benefits to the customer get the remaining 75 percent. If you are selling a car, features include the steering wheel, engine, brakes, and tires. The benefits are that the car will provide safe, affordable, and comfortable transportation to work; I can safely take my kids and their friends to school; I'm going to look great in it; and I am going to be able to travel long distances without worrying about breaking down. People always want to know the features of a car, but more important, they want to know how the car is going to benefit them.

With that understanding, I set out long before we so much as looked at a single demonstration of the Wizetrade products going inside our packaging to get a feel for the approach other companies were taking. I headed over to computer superstore CompUSA to study all of their software box designs. I examined the outside of every software box they had on their shelves. I bought a dozen that caught my eye and brought them back to the office to spread out on my conference table. At this point, I could care less about the contents of the box. It is the outside of the box that matters to me: the look, shape, cardboard thickness, embossing, foil stamping, colors, font sizes, and other design elements. I then called my head graphics designer Megan into my office and asked her which one grabbed her eye first. I tried to come up with what was magic about each of them. I wanted to figure out exactly what made me and everyone else reach up and grab that particular box off the shelf. I can't tell you how many sticky notes I stuck to the outside of a plain white box until I got all of the details figured out. It took a little time, but once I could pinpoint all of the sales elements that worked, I designed the perfect packaging for our software. The perfect packaging of one focused item always translates to your website, collateral material, advertisements, and trade show booth. Pick one, focus, and build it first.

You may think quality packaging isn't important or is too expensive—especially if you are just launching your product— but if you are doing it right, the package will always get you X percent more in sales than a blah brown paper bag. Having that packaging in my hands always helps me find clarity and focus for what is supposed to go inside. Packaging can be a website, brochure, or postcard too—it doesn't have to be a literal box for your product. Focusing on packaging gives me direction and, if I am lucky, an "aha!" moment where it all comes together. A focus on packaging inevitably directs me toward ways in which I need to enhance my product.

Finally, another important secret to remember when creating great packaging is to keep it simple. If you plan to sell your wares, you better find a way to simplify everything so people can understand what they're buying. The bottom line is this: I see the simplicity in everything I do. If I don't, I won't do it.

Never, ever skimp on packaging. Quality packaging will most likely sell your product. Superior packaging will sell your product in your absence. I will never forget opening the packaging of my first iPhone. My mouth fell wide open! I was more intrigued with what Steve Jobs had accomplished with his packaging than I was with the phone itself. I still have the box. It told me clearly that what I was holding in my hand was a BRILLIANT product. If the packaging was this well though-out, just think how well the product must work.

Your packaging determines who you are. It is the game changer at all levels of your business. I bet you're thinking to yourself, "That's great but I don't have an 'eye' or talent for packaging and I certainly can't afford to pay an ad agency or focus group to come up with packaging for me. How can I possibly do this for myself?" YOU

CAN DO THIS no matter what level of artistic talent you may have. Inspiration for quality packaging is all over the place. You simply have to dedicate some time to open your eyes and LOOK.

As strange as this may sound, I find tremendous and FREE inspiration for my packaging ideas from shopping the windows at high-end mall stores and walking the aisles of top grocery and book stores. My core team and I often take field trips to the mall to simply walk down the center and take pictures of cool color combinations, textures, logos, text, and display methods. I once found the perfect color for a trading software box from an Oreo cookie wrapper! It was beautiful foil blue!

It's so easy. However, know that you have to fly in these stores with an "observer's" mindset and not a "shopper's" mindset. Try to walk in a mall and pretend you can't speak or read English and look past the marketing blitz. Just walk down the center of the wings and absorb the overall theme in a window and the path the professional took to get there. You are lucky as you get to capitalize on the fact that these stores are spending hundreds of millions of dollars employing consultants and conducting focus groups to ensure that what they are projecting in their packaging will sell their products. YOU GET IT ALL FREE!!

A Cornell study discovered an uncomfortable truth about children's cereal box packaging and it's not their sky-high sugar content. It's the hypnotic eyes of their cartoon mascots. I think its BRILLIANT packaging! While the people on adult cereals look straight ahead, the researchers found that cartoon tigers (like our friend Tony) and captains (as in Cap'n Crunch) and the like tend to stare downward. This allows the cartoon mascot to gaze right into the eyes of the intended consumer, your kid. This finding makes sense since they also discovered that eye contact increases brand trust by 16%!

Grocers have long been known to place the kids' stuff on lower shelves. But even those shelves can be above many kid's heads. To make up for that, the researchers found that characters like Cap'n Crunch, Tony the Tiger, and Lucky the Leprechaun all look downward at an average of 9.67 degrees. Brilliant packaging! The point is that you can even walk down the cereal aisle in a grocery store and seize millions of dollars' worth of packaging ideas for FREE!

In life, we package ourselves every day by what we choose to wear, which car we drive, our hairstyles, and even where we work. That is the image we project to the world, and it shapes how they perceive us. So you can see why, in business, packaging is everything. Attractive, quality packaging represents who you are as a company and what your product does. If it's done right, your packaging will be impossible to pass up.

ORTHODOX PATH: Finish your product, then work on your packaging (box or website).

SPARKS PATH: Build your packaging (box or website) first . . . everything else will come!

19

Advertising

An effective and relatively inexpensive way to test your product is to run a newspaper ad. I have had tremendous success running simple, traditional ads for whatever it is I want in life. Sure, print advertising is fading away, but use it while you still can. If I am looking for a distributor for one of my products in England, I will run a half-page ad for the product and then clearly state, "Seeking distributor to sell X product." Be bold; express exactly what you are looking for. Despite the worry that our ad will end up as fish wrapping in twenty-four hours, someone always sees our ads and knows someone else who might be interested in doing whatever it is we are asking in the ad. They rip it out, hand it off, and we get what we are looking for. Remember how I met George Thompson? That tiny little ad turned out to be the single best investment I've ever made. And for George, taking the time to answer it paid off, too. A $300 ad turned into a $200 million a year enterprise.

We have run countless ads for various products I've invested in over the years. To this day, it never ceases to amaze me that an ad you and your associates think is perfect can sometimes net horribly dismal results . . . not even a nibble on the line you've cast. In those cases, we end up going back to the drawing board to come up with something completely new and different. We just keep trying until we discover what works. We call it "dialing it in." Knowing what doesn't work is as valuable as knowing what does work.

The most effective ads focus on the benefits of the product you are selling. You would be astonished at how many ads say, "Buy my widget now for $99!" but never tell you how the product benefits you. As a consumer, I want to know all of the reasons I need your product. If you can hook my attention there, you've likely got my sale. Don't ever assume that because you put all the features of your product in your advertisements that the consumer will figure out all the benefits. Benefits are what sell everything. For example, knowing the benefits of a 4-wheel-drive car—I can travel safely in the snow—versus knowing the benefits of a rear-wheel-drive car can help me with my buying decision. I often ask myself and a half dozen people in our office a simple but extremely thought-provoking question: "WHY is someone buying my product?"

This approach is especially important when you are launching a product that isn't branded. As an entrepreneur, the last thing you want to do is build a product that has a name like "Go Daddy" and not be prepared to fund the marketing behind it, such as the outrageously expensive Super Bowl ads and a VIP sexy female race car driver that put them on the map. I applaud Go Daddy for their success; however, most entrepreneurial organizations don't have the financial backing to leap that far out on a limb.

When it comes to branding, be ready to spend a lot of money if you want people to connect the dots. At the very least, make sure you tell your customer what your product does. Splash Media doesn't mean a thing to most people, but they get what we do when they read, "Social Media Solutions®" as the tagline under our logo. If your company name isn't clear, have a great tagline to define your business or product. Also, "TM" or trademark your name as soon as you can. The small TM on a logo is like staking a flag or claim on a mountain top and saying you got there first and everyone back away! Filing a trademark on a name should not cost more than $1,000; it's well worth paying to protect your name and logo. A trademark also allows you to put the TM symbol on your logo, helping your company or product look larger than life—another lesson in the fake it 'til you make it category. Once your TM has been officially accepted and you have paid a fee, you can display the ® by your tagline. (NOTE: While a TM or ® is a good start, it is not the same as the very expensive legal effort to register a copyrighted [©] logo and name that you often see on major brands.)

How many times have you driven past a storefront or billboard that had a clever name but doesn't tell you what it is? You probably wonder to yourself what they do, and you drive on by. They missed the perfect opportunity to sell their wares right then and there. Another company that has entered my universe is a company called MedMen, MedThin, and MedFem—yes, it had three different names! There was a legitimate journey as to why this business had three different names, but no one will ever remember the name of your company/product if the name isn't consistent. In this case, the product and idea were sound, and the company is well on its way to becoming successful despite its original identity crisis. A good name and brand are crucial to the sale of the company down the road, so the first thing I did when I got my hands on that particular entity was change its name to Total Med Solutions. Our plan was to build a dozen locations, dial in the processes, and then sell the company to someone who was interested in having several hundred locations.

I had a ton of fun when Unistar sponsored an Indy race car one season for the Indianapolis 500. We had an outstanding driver (Sam Schmidt), excellent signage all over the car (Unistar Insurance), and we were in the front of the pack for most of the race; the exposure was out of this world. However, the Indy exercise/investment was not intended at all to sell auto insurance. The investment was designed to create trust transference or a bigger-than-life aura to attract more insurance agents to sell our auto insurance. Mission accomplished! We used the photo ops for months after the event and created a buzz that was worth its weight in gold.

It's an uphill battle to create the next Nike swoosh or pull off trying to be the next Coca-Cola. Don't fall so deeply in love with your product that you lose sight of the end game, which is selling your product. Getting people to *think* about your brand is a lofty billion-dollar goal that isn't at all the same as having people *purchase* your products. If you are spending all of your resources and time branding, then you surely aren't out there selling and closing—and you can't possibly be making any money.

That is why when we first launched Splash Media U (University) we used a circa-1990 type plastic shell to hold our educational DVDs. That's what we could come up with fast enough to get our product to market FEP (Fast, Easy, and Profitable). We produced a thousand sets and had sold close to seven hundred units by the time we dialed in the product to our total satisfaction. When we released the same product in new packaging, we called it "Packaging 2.0" so customers would be excited about opening the box and they'd also think, *I want to be a part of this company.*

The point is, don't ever wait for perfection because no one pays for perfection. In my three-and-a-half decades of being an entrepreneur, I have come to understand that perfection is never rewarded. Even if something is absolutely perfect, you won't get paid any more than if it is 85 percent ready to go. Just get your product to market with whatever you have ready. Sparks Speed pays off!

ORTHODOX PATH: Perfect your product, and then release it to the public in a huge campaign.

SPARKS PATH: Perfection is overrated. Get your product just ready enough, and release it slowly to the market to dial in a successful marketing message. Shoot cheap bullets, not expensive cannonballs, at your target.

Business Cards

When I start building a business of any kind, I am thinking every waking moment about ways to construct and present that company so someone will want to acquire it down the road. Thought goes into everything: from the carpet, to the lighting, to the reception area, and right down to the business cards. At Splash Media, we give everyone a business card. It gives them an instant identity and shows that we respect them from the start. Business cards are a confidence booster and a badge of honor.

They are an inexpensive way to express that you are glad your associate is on your team and that you fully believe in him or her.

Think of your business card as an instant ambassador. My goal is to get you to look at my business card—twice. If someone hands me a card that I could build a house out of, I am going to notice it and look again. If you have a flimsy business card, it quietly tells me, "I have no confidence," and "I am not good at what I do." Next time you hand out one of your cards, pay close attention to the response you receive. If someone looks at it, turns it over, holds onto it, and comments, your stock has instantly gone up with that person. If, however, they flip it like a cheap playing card, it's time to get new business cards.

It's really crucial that you not skimp on the quality of this very important item. Suck it up and pay for a heavier card stock. If you can't come up with a good design and logo, pay someone to do it for you, or use one of the several websites available today that allows you to crowdsource logos. Some of these websites allow you to put up as much as a $300 bounty; as a result, dozens of graphic designers fight to create your logo just to win the money. When you get a design you like, you can select it and pay the bounty to the winner. If you're interested in this approach, Google "crowdsourcing logos" to see the various companies you can use.

While I don't mind a colorful card, I prefer that the design elements appear on the front of the card while the back of the card remains clean and white so people can write on it. I often make notes on cards so I can remember where and through whom we met, or anything else I deem important enough to take away from our meeting. Your business card is the first thing people see when you meet and the last thing you leave behind. If you want to be perceived as a real player, you certainly don't want anyone thinking that you hastily printed your cards from a desktop computer!

ORTHODOX PATH: Get inexpensive business cards and print them overnight.

SPARKS PATH: Locate a printer that has extra-thick card stock for your business cards, and emulate the elements of an extremely professional card you have found.

Put It Up Already—Your Website Can't Wait

Get a website up today! Now! Stop fussing and do it already. Everyone around the globe is swapping crowded stores for the one-click convenience of shopping online. Shopping this way has never been safer or more popular. According to a recent global survey conducted by Nielsen, over 85 percent of the world's online population has used the Internet to make a purchase—that's up 40 percent from two years ago. Interestingly, more than half of all Internet users are frequent online shoppers, making online purchases at least once a month.

One of the biggest misconceptions entrepreneurs have about launching a website is that their website has to be perfect. It does not. (Remember, perfection is never rewarded!) When it comes to business, entrepreneurs are helpless romantics—they are in love with their products. To them, no website could ever be good enough to capture the essence and appeal of those products. While that may be true (though probably not), it isn't serving you at all.

To help get you focused and on the right track, ask yourself three questions:

1. Who do I hope will visit my website?

You need to know the demographic of the people you are targeting. If your intended market isn't currently using your site, revisit your online marketing efforts. Knowing who visits your site will help you discover their mindsets and how your product can support their goals. Tailoring your website to their objectives will result in different paths from the home page, with each path offering content differentiated for user needs. A superclean, simple website is all that matters. Keep the one main thing that screams the loudest about your product above the fold (the portion of the screen that you see when opened at first).

2. What do my website visitors look for?

Many companies mistakenly optimize their websites for the content they have, rather than aligning their web content with what customers want. When deciding on your web strategy, find out what information online visitors are seeking—and then shape the content around what users want to find.

3. Are visitors able to find my website and the information they need there? If not, why?

Your site may offer the information users need, but if it's poorly organized, they will never find it. That is the kiss of death for any company. You cannot afford to lose any traffic. Make your site easy to find and navigate by keeping things simple. Don't create domains that aren't reflective of your company name. Splash Media is simply SplashMedia.com. It isn't SMMedia.com, SMedia.com, or any other derivative that could confuse people. Look, if people can't find your site, they most likely won't become customers. A clear domain name is critical to traffic.

Once people are on your site, make sure they can find what they are looking for quickly and easily. How many times have you landed on a site, and out of frustration, signed off and clicked on someone else's site because it was easier to navigate? Studies conducted at the digital research consultancy AnswerLab found that an average of 30 percent to 40 percent of website visitors aren't able to find the information they seek on websites. Common causes include poor navigation, unclear link names, site errors, and technical issues. Consumers don't like to have to play around to uncover the information they need. Eliminating basic usability issues ensures your customers will visit your page . . . and stay!

Look, there are millions of websites in cyberspace; find one you like and replicate it. Put yourself in the position that your consumers will be in once they click on a link to your site. Whatever they see on the screen needs to be powerful because that is most likely the only chance you are going to have to capture them. If you are not the kind of person who can think like the consumer, then put your site in the hands of five people you know, and trust them to give you honest feedback on what they feel when they click into your site. Be willing to hear their thoughts with an open mind so you can make the experience for your customers one that counts.

Having no website broadcasts, "We suck at what we do! We are so lame we have no presence!" To be fair, a good website is a constant work in progress, but today you have no chance of success if you don't have a site at all. Can you afford the time it takes to produce a perfect website? The lost opportunity of waiting until you achieve perfection can be costly—it's the difference between success and failure. If you are launching a business and still don't have a website, stop reading this book and get one up and running today. Getting a basic website up and running should not take more than a few days. Don't try to think of every little detail your site should have on day one. A website truly is a living, breathing part of your business and will evolve as your company evolves. You can't think of everything up front, and you are wasting time trying to do so instead of getting your product to market.

ORTHODOX PATH: Spend six months and thousands of dollars on a website that will be obsolete three months after you launch it.

SPARKS PATH: Find a website style you like and replicate it today with your verbiage. Have it up by Friday, and refine as your message and product evolve.

If you really want to grab someone's attention, a FedEx or UPS package is a very impressive way to send communications and products. Everyone opens a FedEx package. Plus, you can get a bulk rate on their two-day delivery, making it an affordable and value-added marketing tool. I like to use cardboard tubes for mailer marketing as you are guaranteed whatever is inside will be looked at.

Secret Sauce

For your best chances of success, your product must contain something proprietary to your company, something that sets it apart from competitors' products. The primary consumer products I have invested in over the years have been insurance and software. Software is highly documented, proprietary material—the secret sauce—and that's what makes it so valuable. Software is mysterious and never finished because there are always ways to improve upon the existing product. What used to be referred to as a new version is now called an update. When we launch new software programs, we go into it knowing that they are never finished, which means they are really never completely ready for the marketplace. If I had waited to launch any one of our products until it was done and ready, we never would have released a single one.

Remember, lots of companies can sell donuts, but not everyone is Krispy Kreme or Dunkin' Donuts. If you want to separate yourself from those companies, you better have something that makes you different. You guessed it—the donut on a stick.

I never outsource programming because when it comes to software design, you want to own everything. After all, the secret sauce is what you will be selling someday. From the first day you start designing a software program, codebase the source code into a repository (deposit what you program each day into a vault so you are sure to capture all of your data). A lot of new entrepreneurs might undervalue the concept of depositing source code weekly in a vault, but it is a critically important habit to develop.

Once you have the initial packaging and product ready to go, forget walking like an elephant, getting mired down in tests and focus groups. Get to market with what you have in place, and let that be your test. Are people buying it? If not, why not? Don't let anything slow you down. Remember, he who is first to market is king. Time matters! If you know you've got tweaks and changes you want to make, I'm not suggesting you forgo them altogether. Simply start making them while you are in play. Even the biggest companies in the world don't always get it right the first time, but they know you have to get something out there for people to try and to generate feedback. If your product fails or the message to buy is incorrect, at least you will know whether it is fixable or time to cut bait and move on. If you don't throw a line in the water, you will never know if you can catch a fish! Remember, failure to launch is failure to win.

Effective Press Releases

Consumers are hungry for information on future technologies and products. With this in mind, automobile manufacturers market future vehicles, cars that are not yet on the market. Everyone loves to see the yet-to-be released models of the future, even if they're only prototypes. This same thought holds true for everyday business. Early in my career, I learned the value of announcing exciting news to my customers. I discovered that people like hearing about the new and improved products and solutions we are coming up with, and they really want to be kept informed. The bigger my companies get, the more public interest there is in our progress. I started writing press releases out of necessity during my Unistar days. We were growing at such a fast pace that we couldn't keep up with interview requests from the media. Press releases were a quick, inexpensive, easy way to keep the public informed. I also discovered another reason to write a press release: to garner even more interest by offering feature story ideas to reporters. Reporters are more likely to consider a story idea if they first receive the press release, a fundamental tool of public relations work, one that anyone who's willing to use the proper format can use. We employ them for everything—big or small—because they are effective and often bring us business from unexpected places.

A press release, also known as a news release, is a written statement to the media and the public. A press release can announce a range of news items: scheduled events, personnel hires and promotions, awards, new products and services, sales accomplishments, expansion, acquisitions, and other newsworthy tidbits. Press releases are also a road-map to your journey and, if used properly on your website, they give new staff and potential suitors a historical perspective of your success. People are curious and want to know how you got where you are. It gives them a tremendous amount of comfort knowing you have documented what you have done to get you where you are today. I love searching public companies that interest me because they are required to tell the world about everything, and they are prolific press release machines. If I am interested in how a company accomplished a certain goal, I don't go to their financials or scan their home page on their website—I look at their press releases. Press releases give me a chronological path of milestones the company has reached and is proud to share with the entire world. Sure, press releases are chest pounding, but all you need to do is read between the lines and a very clear picture of that company and its key staff will appear.

An effective press release will first have a headline that announces something interesting to grab the attention of readers. It should be brief, clear, and to the point. The headline is an ultra-compact version of the release's key point. Headlines are written in bold and are typically in a larger type size than the rest of the press release text. Conventional press release headlines are present tense and exclude "a" and "the" as well as forms of the verb "to be" in certain contexts. The first word in the press release headline should be capitalized, as should all proper nouns. Most headline words appear in lowercase letters, although adding a stylized small caps style can create a more graphically news-attractive look and feel. Do not capitalize every word.

The second step is to write the body of the release. Tell the story as you want it to appear in all forms of media. Start with the date and city in which the press release originated—this is often referred to as the dateline. The city may be omitted if it will be confusing (for example, if the release is written in Dallas about events in the company's Los Angeles offices). The lede, or first sentence, should grab the reader and say concisely what is happening. The next one or two sentences expand on the lede. Press release body copy should be compact, so avoid using lengthy sentences and paragraphs. Also stay away from repetition, overuse of fancy language, and industry jargon. The first paragraph (two to three sentences) must summarize the press release, and further content must elaborate on it. In a fast-paced world, neither journalists nor their readers will read the entire press release if the start of the article doesn't generate interest.

A great press release answers who, what, where, when, why, and how in a couple of paragraphs. The length of a press release should be no longer than three pages. If you are sending a hard copy, text should be double-spaced. The more newsworthy and interesting you make the copy, the better the chances of its being selected by a journalist for reporting.

ORTHODOX PATH: Hold your "wins" close to your vest and maintain secrecy.

SPARKS PATH: Issue press releases as often as significant milestones occur in anticipation that, in time, a VIP will be excited to learn your chronological path and possibly acquire your company.

Fanning the Flame

Since everything we do in business comes down to selling, it is crucial to fan the flame at every chance. Continually bolster the success of your product. Think of this as another opportunity to sell, sell, sell, so ABC! (See part two for more on learning your ABCs: Always Be Closing!). Slicks or product one-sheets, brochures, flyers, and even free samples are all effective ways to keep people informed and excited about your product.

These marketing tools need to be well planned to create an appealing image that stands out in a crowd. The impact of a single piece of paper or a brochure can mean the difference between losing a sale and closing a sale.

A good one-sheet tells customers everything they need to know about the merchandise. It is a summary primarily used for publicity and sales. Think of a movie poster as a great example of what a product one-sheet should do. It prominently displays the name of the film, the stars, and the key players; then it contains one or two lines that describe the plot. One-sheets or slicks are used in a variety of industries, especially in entertainment. Movie studios and record companies frequently send out one-sheets to promote upcoming releases. The goal of a one-sheet is to spark interest in the product being advertised. In the case of promotional material aimed at the public, the material on the one-sheet may not be incredibly detailed, but it will pique the interest of someone who sees it.

One-sheets are also frequently used in sales so customers have something to take home and read. A car salesman might give out one-sheets for the models clients test-drive, so they can read the material at their leisure. We use slicks as a great way to get to market. Often, we have an urgent or unexpected need to share our story with several hundred people. If you're ever in a similar bind, rest assured that you can have professional one-sheets printed in most cities in a matter of hours.

Designing an effective one-sheet is an art. Personally, I like all of my promotional material to be printed on large, heavy card stock. Consider using larger paper so that after an event, your piece sticks out a few more inches than all the others. I always use bright colors for my collateral materials because I want the recipient to remember our products and services.

Another way I continually fan the flame is to give away free products. Everyone loves free stuff. It amazes me how often people will clamor for things they don't even want just because they are free. At a trade show, never waste money giving away promotional items such as toys and pens. People toss them in a bag and rarely look at them again. Give your pens away to *buying* customers and they will remember you.

Watch people trample one another for a free cookie and hot cocoa. Have you ever seen fans in a ballpark grabbing for a promotional T-shirt thrown into the crowd as if they were angling for something of great value? It's a T-shirt! And how many times have you come home from a charity event thrilled that you have a swag bag full of goodies? Once you open it, more often than not, it's a bunch of stuff you don't want or need, but the companies who provided the products for that bag achieved their goal—to get it into your hands. There's nothing better than word-of-mouth advertising . . . you tell a friend who tells a friend and so on. Often, that word of mouth stems from a product you love and were given for free.

Marketers have always known that giving away free product is one of the best ways to capture a customer. Giving your product away for free cannot be your business model, but it can be a *part* of your business model. If done correctly, free giveaways can increase your market share greatly. If you don't do it correctly, someone else will, and your existing business model will be in serious trouble.

Never use cents in marketing or communicating numbers. For example, if the cost of your product is $395, print, "$395" and not "$395.00." Aside from the cents being irrelevant, you don't want to give the impression that the amount is large. Likewise, if you have a product you are marketing at $1,495, always use the comma to separate the thousand-dollar digit from the others. I often see people omit the comma ($1495), and when that happens, the numbers run together, making the amount look much larger than it is. These details matter in the psychology of a sale.

Free Seminars

The seminar is one of the best tools I have successfully leveraged through the years to promote my various products. My team and I have it down to a science; every detail has been carefully thought out to induce the best response from our attendees. When done correctly, an effective seminar is a technical machine that can alter the chemistry and dynamics of the room and its inhabitants. What I want you to see is what you see. Period. We have had numerous companies ask us to perform seminars for them, and we have historically declined. (Note to self: might there be a business opportunity here?)

Every slide, every PowerPoint page, and every gesture the speaker uses is completely scripted to grab the attention of each attendee. Even the room is designed to create a specific look. For example, I turn the chairs in an inverted V (a chevron shape) so the attendees don't look at flat rows when they walk in the room. I want the people sitting in those seats to see everything within their periphery. I want them to notice when someone else is nodding his or her head up and down in agreement with what our speaker is saying. When the speaker holds up his hand to ask the audience a deliberately leading question, it's also part of our sell—the infectious buy-in we get from the audience. When the speaker asks intentionally affirmative questions, we know your answer is going to be "yes," and you will raise your hand in agreement. By design, we only use the last seven or eight minutes of a ninety-minute presentation to sell our product.

At its peak, GlobalTec Solutions was running eight seminars a week in eight different locations around the country. We used this sales technique to introduce people to our products. One of our biggest draws grew into a highly produced annual convention event we called WizeFEST, an event that was initially created as a thank-you for our customers. I had a precise vision for this event from the start. I wanted it to feel like a Mary Kay rally, where 3,000 fanatical users of our products could gather to meet, mingle, compare notes, and get to know one another. I also knew that if we had all of those paying customers under one giant roof, there was a golden opportunity to create evangelical customers (lifers) and to provide additional training products.

Because Splash Media is the single largest outsourcer of social media services and training, the company sponsors free ninety-minute boot camps that introduce those in attendance— mostly small business owners—to social media and the various methods their company could be benefitting from if they take advantage of Splash Media's social media expertise and offerings. We offer these seminars as a way of bringing together prospective customers who are in search of the same thing—a better understanding of the uses for social media and the positive impact it can have on their business. Once they see what Splash Media has to say about lost opportunities and ways we can help them get on the gravy train, these potential customers walk out of our meeting room believing they need to have our insights, help, and—ultimately— our platform and product, because there is no way they could do it on their own. Now that we've just spent eighty-two minutes selling them by opening their eyes to these missed opportunities, we go in for the close. If the seminar has been done properly and you have given a ton of value, you are rewarded with the ability to pitch the audience something. During the last minutes of the boot camp, the attendees are told that Splash Media can provide exclusive social media services to their business, removing all of the mystery and worry about social media through one special product.

Always serve your customers!

Treat your customers better than you treat family. Customers are the reason you are in business. When customers complain about a product, don't blow them off by telling them you will have to look into the issue and call them back. Use the opportunity to turn those customers around and keep them for life. If there is a challenge, offer a solution. Do whatever it takes so they remember you for that and not for the negative experience that brought them there in the first place. Give everyone on your team the authority to refund a certain amount of money, too. A customer's challenge is your opportunity to win him or her for life.

Seminars can also be used as Trojan horses for another product. We once provided a ninety-minute seminar on social media for the restaurant industry. The guise was to get restaurant owners and managers in a room to learn about the nuances of social media, yet the sponsor of the event actually sold them restaurant management tools instead. The attendees received so much value from the Trojan horse that they didn't have a problem when the sponsor corralled them to sell them something else they never would have come to hear about. Everyone wins!

Like Striking Gold

Recurring revenue is the Holy Grail for companies whose products can support it. It is the portion of a company's revenue that is highly likely to continue in the future and create tremendous enterprise value for the company. This is revenue that is predictable and stable, revenue that can be counted on with a high degree of certainty in years to come. For example, a cable company that has millions of customers paying monthly fees could consider a large portion of its monthly revenues to be recurring. This is a highly desirable quality for a company to have because suitors often love recurring revenue more than the product itself.

A valuable, sellable company can demonstrate how its business will continue to thrive after the founder is gone. One of the best ways to show this is through the existence of long-term contracts that guarantee an ongoing stream of revenue, subscription services, membership clubs, and evergreen products people need to replace regularly, such as printer toner. If I had a product that sold for \$1,200 flat-out or a product that sold for \$99 a month for a year, I'd sell the \$99-a-month product all day long.

No, I have not lost my mind. This is Sparks Psychology 101, and the reason is perception. To a company buyer, perception is reality. Your buyer would rather see recurring revenue (or continuity revenue) than a one-off sale. Also, you leave something on the table for the buyer to sink his teeth into the day after he purchases your company.

There's a wide range of businesses that can be turned into a recurring business model. First, ask yourself a few questions to see if your idea fits:

1. Would customers willingly pay a monthly or annual fee for the latest version of my product?

2. Is there an educational component of my product that I could sell as a monthly subscription?

3. Does the consumer need to buy my product regularly to keep another product working?

If you can't answer yes to these three questions, then you need to make sure you can demonstrate that you have a systematic and predictable way to reach your customers.

ORTHODOX PATH: Take 100% of
the annual revenue up front.

SPARKS PATH: Take the annual revenue in
twelve monthly payments to leave recurring
revenue on the books for a potential acquirer.

Another great way to create a high sense of value for your company is to have several patent-pending products in your arsenal. A patent pending is optically as important as a patent. A patent pending telegraphs that you have confidence in your product and think it is proprietary and unique (your secret sauce). You can patent almost anything, so make sure you don't lose an opportunity to capture that added value along the way. Remember, you want to be building value for your company every day.

Use Strong Communication

Communication sounds like a "duh" topic; however, if you miss this rather obvious need, you will indeed fail. Overcommunicating to your team is crucial. It doesn't matter if you have one person or one hundred people on your team. I have been a serial entrepreneur all of my life, and it still amazes me that no matter how much overcommunicating I do, there is always someone on my team who doesn't get the information I'm sharing. As a leader in your organization or as a leader on a specific project, your number one goal is to make sure everyone is rowing in the same direction, at the same time. I will often send out an email with bullet points that read, "In the spirit of overcommunicating . . ." just to reiterate my expectations.

When you overcommunicate, you accomplish so much more than simply delegating; you let your team know you are the kind of leader who wants to think of everything so they can count on you. You are also sending a message that you are thinking about the company's projects all of the time. Believe me—that kind of comfort gives your teammates in the field tremendous security in knowing you genuinely care. They will aspire to work hard and will go out of their way to produce for you.

It's important to understand that communication can sometimes be a double-edged sword. Your team may not need to know absolutely everything. Certain details about your company should be kept to yourself or to your inner circle. For example, saying something such as, "I might not be able to make payroll next month if these sales don't happen," and sending out any type of communication with an "if" in it never plays well for anyone. First, a lot can happen with an "if," and often the worry you convey is more debilitating to your staff than it is helpful. Second, everyone wants to know that he or she is working in a stable environment . . . that his or her job isn't hanging by a string. An effective leader can bring the team through the hard times without placing the worry and concern on their already overloaded shoulders.

ORTHODOX PATH: Share communications sparingly. Only the person you are speaking to receives the communication.

SPARKS PATH: Overshare communication with the management team often. CC your email communications often!

Selling in a Down Economy

Many entrepreneurs go into business planning for the good days, but few prepare for the unexpected, such as a downturn in the economy. Anyone who started a business between 2008 and 2012 has been dealing with a recession, the highest levels of unemployment in our country's history, and consumers who have been crushed by their financial advisers and who won't part with their hard-earned dollars unless they have no other choice. What does this mean to you as a business owner?

Work smarter and harder! Sell more. Just do it!

In the corporate world, there is no more important or valuable asset than your sales team. They are crucial to your company's success or failure. I love salespeople and have a tremendous respect for what they do because a great sales force will always generate income for a company. Even in a down market, sales are what keep a company afloat. If you're running a company, you must carefully explain the importance of sales to every single person in your business, from the receptionist to the CEO. Make sure everyone knows he or she is a part of the sales process. We are all selling at every point throughout the life of any relationship.

Each team member has to eat, sleep, and breathe sales. I have seen too many situations in which the sales staff carries the brunt of a bad economy, making it their sole responsibility to bring in all of the business. Instead of relying on his or her sales team to save the company from failing, a great leader will see an opportunity to refocus current talent and help bring in new business. Maybe this means that an administrative assistant redirects her talent toward blogging on behalf of what you are selling or toward listening on social media sites for the trends and needs people are talking about, as they apply to your product. Soon enough, bingo! She might snag a lead and can immediately let the sales team know about it.

The great motivational speaker Zig Ziglar once said, "Money is not important; however, it is right up there with oxygen." If you want your team to truly feel like they're a part of the process, make sure to share updates on sales with the entire staff. You don't have to give exact dollar amounts. You can inspire your team by saying, "We sold nine widgets in the past twenty-four hours!" Everyone rallies around reaching a sales goal. It doesn't matter if a person is a Type A or Type D personality. Everyone needs to understand that sales are the reason for the job in the first place.

In a down economy, you have to generate more sales and increase your enterprise value. By excelling in a down economy, your company will have propelled light-years ahead of its competition by the time the economy turns back around—and it always turns around. In tough times, I have often preached, "Don't worry—we can sell our way out of this." And for the most part, we do.

In a down economy, I often see companies shed all or part of their sales team, something that truly boggles my mind. I've never understood the thought process behind a corporate restructuring that cuts a sales force. Sales are the company bloodline. Nothing happens if nothing is sold. NEVER, EVER let go of your sales staff. The last person standing should be a salesperson!

Sales are the only thing you have that can pull you out of all kinds of murky water. If you are faced with having to make cutbacks through layoffs, consider other departments such as support personnel or marketing. If you've got to cut back on personnel, ask yourself who you can live without. Can you answer your own phones? We all have to tighten our belts in a down economy, but don't throw the baby out with the bathwater.

A down economy is the most crucial time to dig deep and think out of the box. One way to accomplish this goal is to set and broadcast a specific day and time when you and your team are all going to come together (perhaps within seventy-two hours). When you meet again, create a list of every idea, no matter how big or small it may sound, on a dry erase board and support it with an action plan. Then, mix everyone up for an afternoon so the shipping clerk is with the fulfillment team or the salespeople are with the administration group. Make your team a part of the solution, get them to embrace the challenge (notice I didn't say problem), and they'll truly be endeared to you and your vision for a long time. People are naturally drawn to supporting a cause as long as they feel as if they are making a valuable contribution.

It's critical to be brutally honest with your team in a down economy—you aren't hiding anything from them anyway, so the best course of action is to be realistic and embrace realities as a team. Reassure your team that their jobs are not in jeopardy as long as you can figure out ways to sell more products and deliver better service to your customers. If you can coach them through this difficult time and they can find creative ways to rise to the occasion, they will be loyal associates for years to come.

A down economy is a perfect time to figure out a way to give something of value away free, such as free software, free training, free coaching, or a free cheeseburger with the purchase of a cheeseburger. Free is good if you have a great flagship product.

The secret to getting through lean times is to eliminate unnecessary bureaucracy and paperwork obstacles so you can get the job done. I realize processes are important at times; however, getting that business in the door before your competitor does is a matter of survival these days. JUST DO IT! Implement an action plan and open the gates today.

ORTHODOX PATH: Let salespeople go first in a down economy to cut costs.

SPARKS PATH: Salespeople are the last to be let go in a down economy. There's not much for your other staff to service if you don't have sales.

Pruning

Did you know that cutting limbs and branches off a tree will actually encourage more fruit from that tree and possibly save it from disease? Pruning trees and bushes is critical to a fruit farmer's success.

Listen up! This is a lesson I learned late in my career, and I am hoping you can learn from my mistake. Entrepreneurs are typically hard-charging folks who say "yes" to a lot of stuff simply because they want it all. I was guilty of relentlessly saying "yes" to just about everything because I was afraid I was going to miss something. We think that the next person we meet or the next gizmo we look at will be the one that makes or breaks us. Hard-chargers like us simply do not have brakes.

There are thousands of books (mine included) written to help you do more, get more, and make more money; however, you don't see books on eliminating the noise and clutter in your life. It's human nature to amass clutter and noise. We all take on way more than we can chew. We are inundated with technology, spouses, kids, church, sports, philanthropy, constantly changing business rules (e.g., Obamacare), doctor appointments, birthdays, associate challenges, changing tax laws, meetings, and general commitment overload. It's kind of crazy how much we fear losing out on something.

Well, the fear of losing out on something finally caught up with me and started affecting my health. I work out four to five times a week, I'm not overweight, I spend a lot of time outdoors, I don't smoke, I get regular checkups, and I eat fairly well. As far as vices, I do love a good glass of oaky chardonnay, I smoke an occasional cigar, and I try to eat one juicy cheeseburger a week. I think I'm fairly healthy, right? Well, out of the blue about two years ago, the stress of a hard-charging entrepreneurial life finally caught up with me. I got a bizarre rash. It just appeared one day and said, "Deal with it, brother."

This ailment was a real wake-up call! I went to seven doctors—if you count a shrink and an acupuncturist—and no one could tell me what it was or what the cause was. It wasn't an all-over-the-body kind of rash either. It attacked certain areas, like my chest, stomach, thighs, and lower back, and it raged on for months, itching and burning. I tried everything from doctor's prescriptions to home remedies, and nothing helped until, out of sheer exhaustion, I started eliminating stuff from my schedule and life. I started pruning and, alas, the rash started going away. I eliminated a few businesses that were sucking the life out of me. I eliminated real estate holdings that had too many moving parts. I eliminated all but three magazine and newspaper subscriptions. I even pruned my closet of everything I had not worn in nine months. I stopped taking meetings that I knew I was taking just to be polite. I stopped sitting on boards, and I started saying "no."

Pruning just might have saved my life! I encourage and challenge you to start pruning in your life today. Cut off everything that is not bearing fruit. Pruning gave me time to listen, time to think, and time to breathe. I am having a lot more fun and making more money because I can truly focus.

ORTHODOX PATH: Take every meeting—
you never know what might come of it.

SPARKS PATH: Take only meetings with
defined agendas, and then decide if they're
going to bear fruit or not. If not, prune!

30

Break It Up

In 1976, I was making just enough money from my job at Freed's Furniture to buy myself a used, canary yellow Oldsmobile Rally 350. It was the coolest car I had ever owned. It had a custom paint job with a black hood, beautiful chrome tie-downs, and a thick black stripe on the side panels. The engine purred like a cat and was pure muscle. The car was assembled by a car fanatic friend I had met in Dallas; he got tired of the car and was ready to sell it to me for $1,750. My car had a killer spoiler fin on the back that looked like a graceful stingray swimming in the ocean. The exhaust pipes and wheels were customized and chrome-plated. Think of the movie *Shaft*, and you'll get the picture. To me, my car was a rolling symphony orchestra. No matter where I drove it, people would stop and ask me all kinds of questions about it. Others would pull up to me and ask me to race! It was flattering, and my car was super-fast, but I wasn't the racing kind of guy so I would just thank them and rumble on.

A few years later, it was time for me to hit the road selling furniture, and I decided my car wasn't quite the image I needed to portray when I pulled up to a high-end furniture store. I ran an ad in *The Dallas Morning News* to sell it and must have had twenty-five people come to look at it. All of the offers I had on it were below $1,000, which was considerably less than what I had paid for it. (Strangely, today it would sell in auction for over $100,000!) I was really disappointed because I had been sure I'd get at least $2,500 for it because so many people had loved it when I was driving it. I really needed the down payment for a new car.

Then one day a guy about my age pulled alongside me and asked me to pull over so he could talk to me about my car. We pulled into an active 7-Eleven parking lot. He said he was building a car and really needed some parts I had on my car. I asked, "Are you crazy?" He said he needed the spoiler fin, and he'd give me $750 for it because they don't make those anymore. I needed the money for my down payment, and so I decided to let him have it with one stipulation: he had to fill the holes and repaint my trunk lid from the marks the fin had put in the paint job. He agreed and I got my $750. He said he had a friend of his who might be interested in my wheels. I said, "Let's see how this spoiler fin situation goes down first."

Ten days later, another guy called me and said his friend had just bought a cool spoiler fin from me, and now this guy wanted to see the chrome wheels if I were willing to discuss selling them. Everything went well with the fin so I thought, *Why not?* The guy showed up and, after a bit of haggling, he ended up offering me $1,000 for all four wheels and tires. I was thinking, *This is pretty cool. I'm one check away from getting all my money back from my original investment, and I still have my car.* I said, "Sure, I'll do it, but you have to get me standard Oldsmobile wheels and good tires first." That evening he showed up with some decent-looking wheels and good tires to swap for my custom chrome mags. Two hours later, he drove off, and I stood there with $1,750 cash and my car still in the driveway. It was crazy cool!

The next day I drove my Rally 350, which had now been slightly modified, to the Oldsmobile dealership and asked them what they would give me for a trade-in of this muscle car for a brand new Oldsmobile I had already negotiated a fair price for. After they test-drove my car and checked it out, the manager came back and said, "We will give you $1,250 for your Rally 350."

I was ecstatic! I happily agreed to their offer and drove home with a brand-new Oldsmobile that I was able to put $3,000 down on because I had been willing to break up my asset. And I drove my Rally 350 for two years basically for free! It turns out my asset (car) was worth more broken apart than it was as a whole.

I have since used this tactic in business on several occasions. Companies often morph into several products due to necessity. For example, Splash Media, LP was born as a social media agency and, due to necessity, we built an accredited online university in the process. Each company is run separately and will be divested separately; however, had we kept them together, we would not have attained nearly the value as a whole.

ORTHODOX PATH: Keep the company assets as one business unit.

SPARKS PATH: Break up the top tier assets of a company to maximize value to multiple potential acquirers.

You may have noticed that throughout this book I never use the word "employee" to refer to people who work for me, as it screams subservient. Instead, I use partner, associate, team member, or staff because I want my team to row the boat with me and not for me. Setting an example as a partner is the key to maximizing the output of your team members. You never want to be a dictator; you simply want to be the dude (or dudette) in charge. Dictators rarely get ideas from their teams. Make sure you reward ideas when they are brought to you. And when it comes to how you treat your team, my philosophy is simple: treat everyone with respect. Praise publicly and reprimand in private.

Finding the Heart of a Transaction

When I get involved in a negotiation, I go into it as though I am conducting a friendly transaction as opposed to fighting an adversarial battle. It's a lot like playing a high-stakes game of poker, when every player at the table has the potential to impact the outcome. For me, thinking of it as a transaction connects the dots in a far more positive way. I don't even like to use the word "deal" because I feel like it cheapens what you are trying to accomplish, as if you were getting a deal on a used car.

When it comes to making a transaction, most people get bogged down in too many details. During a negotiation, many little things can happen that might seem important at the time, but in the long run, they aren't worth fighting over. It is crucial to maintain focus on the purpose and goals. For example, in an acquisition of a company, so many people fall into the common trap of focusing on the little things until something I call deal fatigue sets in. Lawyers and accountants are the biggest causes of deal fatigue because they sometimes get fiercely fixated on the wrong things, such as ongoing employee benefits and compensation plans. Yes, these are important topics, but they shouldn't overshadow the bigger picture. Everyone should be focused on the heart of the transaction because he or she wants the deal to go through. Paying too much attention to the minutiae often results in losing the very thing you are trying to gain.

Deal fatigue eventually sets in during nearly every merger or acquisition I do. In the negotiating room, it's critical to have personalities that work well together. During my sale of GlobalTec

Solutions, the buyer and I agreed that we would intervene the minute the attorneys started "peeing in the pool" and screwing up the transaction. Often, the buyer and I would have to excuse ourselves to go in another office. The minute we shut the door, we would decide how it was going to go down. I'd win one and he'd win one; I'd win the next and he'd win the next. The attorneys and accountants were clearly brilliant people; however, they had all lost the true meaning of the heart of the deal. We got it done, but it was only because we didn't let the tail wag the dog.

What's most important is to remember the heart of the transaction. What is it that you are trying to accomplish? What's the desired end result?

There's a story that says trappers in South America catch monkeys by tying a loosely woven basket with a bottlenose opening to a tree. The opening is only about two inches in diameter—just large enough to slip a few bananas inside. The bananas lure the monkeys to the basket. When a monkey puts his hand in the two-inch opening, he grabs the banana, but when he tries to pull his arm out, it gets stuck because holding the banana prevents him from being released. All the monkey would have to do is let go of the banana and he'd free his arm, but most won't do that because they want the banana. The monkey is willing to lose everything to get one banana.

When you're negotiating, learn to let go of the banana, and I promise you will always come to some common ground. I let go of bananas every day to accomplish what I set out to do. I don't overanalyze in those situations; I acknowledge that the banana is much more important to you than it is to me, and I let go so you can have it, and I can meet my ultimate goal.

As with my ability to see things before they are built, I have also been blessed with the inexplicable ability to see the future in transactions. I can always see the bigger picture, and believe me, there is always a bigger picture. Not long ago, I was negotiating to sell part of Agency Matrix, one of my software companies. This company produces affordable insurance agency management software that enables users to effectively manage their insurance agency business, their staff, and their office from anywhere. My goal wasn't really to sell the company at this point; however, I knew the buyer had a significant client base, and that he and I together could benefit substantially from our services and each other's assets. (A classic case of two plus two equaling ten!) We already had about a thousand insurance agents using our software, but the buyer had 5,000 more agents buying his insurance products. He needed something that we had, and we needed something that he had, so in this process there was an opportunity . . . but only if I let go of the banana so both of us would thrive. I made a respectable profit for my percentage; however, I will clearly do many times better with my remaining equity interest as I did with the first transaction. This gave me two bites of the apple! We closed the transaction, and several other opportunities have come forth with the same party since. In essence, my letting go of that one banana set us all free to flourish.

My success can be attributed best to the fact that I am someone who doesn't lose focus or sight of the ultimate goal, which is to bring everything back to center until we can close the transaction. If you focus intently on the ultimate goal and on the heart of the transaction, you will be able to go back and do business with these people again and again. For example, the guy who purchased Agency Matrix from me was a serious acquisition candidate more than fifteen years earlier, in my Unistar insurance days. We did each other right then, and that afforded us the opportunity to circle back more recently to take another stab at success together.

I now own a substantial portion of the entire operation he spent two decades building.

I'm constantly amazed at how entrepreneurs in the *Shark Tank* show miss the biggest point of all. The goal isn't to get $100,000 for 10 percent of your company. The goal is to get one of the profoundly successful sharks to become the ambassador of your product to ensure your success! For gosh sakes, pay the shark $100,000 for 49 percent of your company just to be in the same room with him or her!

ORTHODOX PATH: Fight tooth and nail for every deal point in an acquisition negotiation.

SPARKS PATH: Keep your eye on your goal, and let go of the things that don't matter in the long run! Don't let the tail wag the dog in negotiations. Own the room!

Pigs Get Fat, Hogs Get Slaughtered

On the floor of my office, I keep a life-size ceramic pig to remind me that pigs get fat and hogs get slaughtered. This business philosophy has served me well over the years. I have built a lot of companies, and I have sold a few for what some would define as less than market value, yet it was enough and it felt right to me. When people buy companies from me, they genuinely believe they can make them better, and that they, in turn, can sell them for more than what they paid me.

Every time I sell a company, I leave a little something on the table. I could grab more, but I don't because I know the difference between a windfall and a downfall. Unfortunately, there are many people who do not. Greed will kill a transaction quicker than anything.

I was once approached by a seminar marketer who wanted to sell Wizetrade software at his events. He ran one of the largest speaking tours in the world and was looking for new products. There was a tremendous sense of urgency when he called because he knew he was missing out on an opportunity to increase revenue from the captive audience members who came to his seminars by the tens of thousands! I knew that he attracted some of the biggest names in the world as speakers (former presidents, world leaders, and sports celebrities), so I thought it might be interesting to see how we could join forces for at least an event or two.

We agreed to meet at his offices in Florida to discuss various possibilities. (You will read in Spark Thirty-Three why meeting on someone's home court is never a good idea!) He spent half a day beating me up on what he thought was a fair split on the sale of our product. He wanted to retain 96 percent of the proceeds, leaving me with a whopping 4 percent. I laugh out loud to this day! Yep, you read correctly—96 percent of the sale proceeds to him, and 4 percent of the sale proceeds to me. I was shocked at his offer, as I had already invested millions of dollars in my products. I had over one hundred staff members back in Dallas, maintaining the software and handling sales and customer service. I had a customer base already using my products, for gosh sakes! And I retained *all* of the profits! There was no incentive for me to make this transaction happen. I simply could not understand his rationale in this venture. I knew he was in a very needy position, but his negotiating tactics made it terribly undesirable to be in business with this man.

After hearing his ideas, I decided to lay out my thoughts. After all, I had made the trip with the intention of creating opportunity for both of us. I put my case out in front of him—a case I thought made sense. My concept was that my team would provide the product as well as the ongoing customer service, while he provided the venues and the people in attendance. From my perspective, this was a fifty-fifty venture. We each had our out-of-pocket expenses, but any way you sliced it, the split had to be reasonable or there was simply no reason to agree to it. We spent several hours trying to hash out a fair and equitable transaction. He was being a hog by asking for a massive percentage while leaving only a few crumbs for us. We ended up with a 70 percent share going to him and the remaining 30 percent to me, but only as a three-time test. I let go of the banana because I wanted to go to school and see how he did what he did. I figured it was worth entering into a break-even situation for me to get more customers in my database and to learn everything I could about his seminar business, which has since paid off manyfold in my career.

Looking back, I wasn't surprised when I heard that he eventually made a disastrous agreement with a competitor of ours. When you make a land grab, you can't expect it to turn out well for everyone involved. You have to leave something on the table so the buyer, customer, or whomever you are dealing with is getting a fair shake, too. No one wants to feel taken advantage of, ripped off, or worst of all, deceived. There's usually plenty of profit to keep everyone fat without waking up and suddenly finding yourself headed to the slaughterhouse.

ORTHODOX PATH: Over-negotiate
and grab the last penny!

SPARKS PATH: Leave a little on the table.
The deal is done and everyone wins!

There Is No Home Court Advantage

When I am negotiating, I prefer to hammer out the terms of the agreement someplace other than in the prospective buyer's home court. For whatever reason, people feel like they have an advantage if they can get you on their turf. They actually get cocky about it, so I find it is always better to meet in a neutral space, such as an airport, hotel lobby, or restaurant. I like airports best, as they give you a sense of energy and speed. Airports have an atmosphere of "go, go, GO," so they help move discussions along. At airports, you have planes to catch . . . which usually helps set the pace as well. If at all possible, try to avoid being in a tight space with walls in all directions, such as conference rooms or meeting rooms. An open environment gives everyone the freedom to move around and completely lightens the tensions. In the end, both parties do much better because of it.

Likewise, negotiating in your home court doesn't work well either, because the other party comes into your offices a bit intimidated, thinking you've got some type of leverage over them, when the reality is that you don't. The impact can be extremely detrimental to the transaction—even derailing it—because it raises everyone's defenses.

If at all possible, I prefer to sit at a round table. If a rectangular table is the only option, I try never to sit on the end. I want to be in the center because it makes me feel as though I'm more a part of the transaction and not a polarizing force. I don't want to leave the wrongful impression by sitting at the head of the table, I'm dictating terms. The ideal scenario is to have a room with lots of windows and a round table so that there is no head seat for anyone. It brings a feeling of equality to the negotiation.

Negotiations naturally make people nervous, which leads us to wanting as much space as we can possibly get. This is why most people tend to sit across the table from each other. This is the worst thing you can do! When you sit across from someone, you naturally divide the table in half so that half becomes your space and half becomes the other person's space.

Space plays a big role in negotiations. You have a definite space bubble you carry around you. If you trust people, you let them into your space. If you don't, things can quickly become adversarial. When negotiating, make sure you have a room with enough space for each person to have elbow room. Once a person's body space is invaded, he or she will stop thinking rationally and instead put energy into getting the personal space back! If that happens, the negotiation will most likely fail to close.

ORTHODOX PATH: Negotiate in a windowless attorney's office.

SPARKS PATH: Negotiate in a public place with a round table and lots of windows.

Did you know that when something piques your interest, your pupils will dilate up to four times their normal size? This shows excitement and interest, and we rarely know we are doing it. If during negotiations, a person's pupils dilate, it means he's interested in the opportunity—even if he says he isn't. At that point, hold to your original stance and ask him what he likes most about the transaction. If his pupils contract, you know he's genuinely skeptical of your offer. That's the time either to sell him hard or back away.

Body Language

I've become an expert at studying people's body language, especially during negotiations. Once you learn to read body language, you can see what a person is thinking but not saying. All of us have a "tell"—a physical sign we reveal if we agree or disagree with others, or if we are bored, interested, upset, angry, or confused. When I am excited about something and I'm sitting down, my knee begins to bounce. If we are ever in a negotiations together, don't use that tell against me!

Body language is an instant message of how things are going. When I enter a meeting and someone is sitting at the table and his or her arms are crossed, that usually means there's a problem. That gesture is telegraphing that defenses are up and the person is closed off. You will never get what you are seeking out of that person he or she is being so cautious and resistant. During meetings, there is always information coming at you that you should be filing away. Some classic examples of these telltale signs are switching legs from one side to the next, adjusting or flipping a neck tie, picking lint off clothing, looking up at the ceiling or away from you, crossing and uncrossing arms, looking at fingers, drumming fingers on the table, and turning the meeting agenda facedown. When someone refuses to look you in the eyes during a conversation by either glancing down or beyond you, she is likely trying to avoid confrontation or isn't confident in what she is saying. One move that really gets under my skin is when someone puts his foot up on a conference table. First, it's incredibly rude. Second, it telegraphs that this person is arrogant, he doesn't care about what you're saying, and his ego is way out of check. None of those are signs that things are going well.

I make it a point to be aware of my body language in meetings because I know people are paying attention in much the same way I do. I like to be engaging by presenting myself as open, warm, and welcoming, so I avoid showing signs that might suggest I'm feeling any other way. I will make it a point to look a person in the eye when I am speaking so he or she knows I am secure and comfortable with the things I am communicating.

A Dead Giveaway

The following body signs are important ones to watch for when negotiating. They are based on the European–American Culture and the research work of Desmond Morris, Allan Pease, and Julius Fast, to name a few.

These body signs are guidelines, not absolute truths. When you see a sign, stop and ask questions to make sure you are correctly interpreting the message that person is conveying. Body language is tied to our thoughts and not our words, which is why you can sometimes get mixed signals from people. When in doubt, listen to the body language, not the words.

Here are a few signs that a person is listening and absorbing what you are saying:

- **Hand on Cheek.** This gesture indicates evaluation and genuine interest. The person likes what you have to say and is taking it all in and assessing it. This is a great time to ask leading questions to draw the person out and to hear his or her thoughts.

- **Chin Stroking.** If someone is doing this while you're talking, he is likely making a decision. Don't interrupt his process! Watch for the body language signal that immediately follows. Does he lean back and cross his arms? Those are "no" gestures. If he leans forward, keep quiet and let him talk first.

- **Head Tilt.** This small gesture indicates genuine interest. If you tilt your head while listening to someone else speak, you might be surprised to find you will actually become a better listener.

Ask "Why?" Often

It's important to question everything during a transaction because it's your greatest opportunity to gain crucial and relevant information. Asking "Why?" during a transaction sounds simple, but often people lose sight of the value in doing so. If done in a nonaggressive manner, asking "Why?" comes off as humble rather than arrogant. You never want to ask why as if you already have all of the answers. No one likes a know-it-all! It turns people off, especially during negotiations. Even if you are the smartest person in the room, there is no benefit to proving it to everyone else. The more humble and laid back your demeanor, the further you will go.

It's human nature to want to help people, and when you ask "Why?" you are asking for help. For example, a simple question such as, "Tell me why you market your product only through social media. Why don't you use television, the newspaper, or radio?" sends a message of wanting clarity on something. It empowers the other party to express his or her thoughts and ideas with a nonthreatening response.

Even if you think you know the answer, let her tell you her reasons because you will learn so much more from her response than you already thought you knew. If you continue to ask "Why?" you will keep getting more details and information, some of which can lead to red flags. It's amazing how easy it is to get people to talk by asking that one little question. The simplest observations are revealed if you just let the other parties talk and talk.

If I ever notice that someone at the table is getting nervous or agitated when I'm talking out the details, I stop and ask, "What are your thoughts on this?" "Do you agree with that statement?" "What ideas do you have?" or "What challenges do you think we face with this new idea?" These types of questions are disarming and will help keep the transaction moving forward.

Use Hypotheticals

As a way of extracting additional information, I often create hypothetical situations during conversations I have every day. Hypotheticals come up in all types of situations and can be used as a tremendous tool for communicating your point. For example, if I'm speaking with one of our software designers, I would say to him, "Hypothetically, I want our software to have a similar look and feel to XYZ software." You can't assume that everyone will read your mind, so speaking hypothetically helps make things easier to understand and really brings your point and message home.

Remember that information and communication are gold—especially during an acquisition negotiation. In this case, I might say something such as, "When Google bought Zagat, the company promised to build a larger web presence. Hypothetically, if we were to acquire your company, we could do the same." Saying this gives the other party confidence and comfort in you because it's like showing them a road map to the future.

Watch for Too Many Concessions

When gathering information, note whether the other party is making too many concessions. This type of quick-to-give behavior telegraphs a message of desperation and should be an automatic red flag. There's a reason the other party is giving up so much so fast. Imagine walking into a car dealership and making an offer on a vehicle, which the salesman immediately accepts. There's no push back, no counteroffer—just a quick agreement to your bid. You might believe you're walking away with a great car deal, but the salesman knows he has just unloaded a lemon.

It's a natural instinct for people to want to hold on to as much as they can, so if a seller is openly and freely offering you concessions and incentives during a negotiation, remember that lemon! What are you missing? What information does the seller have that you don't? This is crucial to know before moving forward. Start asking, "Why?" until you uncover what it is you're seeking. The truth always has a way of coming out, especially if you can get the seller to talk. Once you find out what it is, you can either work through it or swiftly walk away.

Identify Weaknesses!

One of the reasons I actively seek to acquire interests in companies is that I have a natural instinct for finding businesses that desperately need what I have to offer—usually capital and extra services. If you can identify the weaknesses in an entity before going after it, you will be armed and ready to go into the transaction and make it happen. Know what they want/need, and you can more effectively sell yourself, your company, and its products/services.

When I negotiated with Paul Slack to acquire WebDex, I offered a complete mix of services, including IT, accounting, legal and sales departments, a state-of-the-art television production studio, a leading social media network, and a campus full of professionals who were ready, willing, and able to take that company to the next level in business. That was nothing short of music to Paul's ears because these were all services WebDex was lacking. Without them, the company wasn't going to grow any further, so he needed someone like us. Knowing his needs made our position worth its weight in gold. Likewise, Paul knew our interests and ended up selling me on the reasons we should be under one banner. That kind of mutual understanding is what led me to acquire his company.

Be a Great Listener

The real skill in asking a good question is that it requires you to become a great listener. An effective private investigator knows how to hear, see, and observe everything beyond the words being spoken. If you're busy telling everyone in the room everything you know, you aren't listening for clues about what you still need to learn. One of the great secrets to success is being an observant listener.

Never underestimate the benefits of keeping an open mind and experiencing new and exciting possibilities. You never know where your next great idea might come from. The key is to learn quickly, listen, and observe. Listening and observing are a powerful combination.

Be Nice and Likable

"You catch more bees with honey." "Kill them with kindness." "Let go of your ego." These adages are ones we have all heard and understood, yet many people fail to live by them. The best way to get a transaction done is to be nice, likable, and humble.

I once had a businessman who was buying one of my companies sign his emails with "Hugs, Alex." This guy is six feet two, 220 pounds, and wasn't crossing a line; he was simply saying, "This is challenging now, but we will thrive when it is over." It always made me smile when he did that. These traits pay off in enormous dividends because you will always win, even if you don't come to terms. This doesn't mean you have to go overboard showering the seller with elaborate gifts. Just be willing to talk about her or her family, interests, and hopes for the future . . . anything you can find to disarm the other person and create a comfortable environment.

Don't Be an Ass

Much of the outcome of any negotiation is based on how you feel about the other person and how the negotiation process is evolving. Some people will come into my office and try to flex their muscles by being cocky or obnoxious instead of gracious and humble. There are those people who want to bully me into a decision. When someone comes into a meeting all fired up and ready for battle, I know I am dealing with a colossal ego. This is the same person who comes to a dinner party and has to be the smartest guy in the room. That kind of aggressive behavior is such a turnoff, especially when it comes to negotiating.

I don't believe there is any room for asses in business. Even though negotiations can become challenging, you always get back what you give. Try being an ass to your vendors and associates for a couple of weeks and see how far that gets you. You will elicit the same results if you act like a total jerk during a negotiation. It's also important that you don't let anyone else be an ass on your behalf.

I once had to pull my attorney out of a room to tell him to back off because he was about to blow it! He was killing us with his know-it-all attitude and arguments over little things that didn't matter to me at all. I asked him to go back in the room and let other people come up with answers so we could salvage the transaction. In the end, you gain absolutely nothing from this type of behavior. Despite your best efforts to keep things calm and reasonable, if things are still spiraling out of control because of someone else's ego, get that person to leave and deal only with the principal. Just stop the train. It's always better to do your transactions principal to principal, but if you're dealing with an attorney, accountant, CFO—or anyone else in authority—whose personality makes your skin crawl, clear through that quickly, or the transaction will go south.

Meet the Family

In any transaction, I require a level of patience that, as a rule, I don't have . . . but I dig deep to find. Other people's timelines often aren't the same as yours. An acquisition or sale can be an emotional experience for the party giving up his or her company. Many times, people feel as though they are losing a child but know that if the transaction isn't completed, they will be out of business in time. Because of these intense feelings, it's crucial to meet the spouse of the principal you're dealing with. I like to meet the spouse as early as possible so I can share with that significant other my reasons for acquiring the company. This kind of interaction helps disarm the emotions that take place in the home and that you might otherwise have no control over.

A gentleman once came to me with a half-baked software product (which ultimately became Agency Matrix) he wanted to show me. I liked the space, I liked the guy, and I liked the software product he had developed so far. I knew him from my Unistar days, so I was comfortable with him from the start. He needed me or someone to take him to the next level, and it wasn't going to happen without his company's folding into my system. However, his biggest challenge in selling me the software company was his wife's hesitance to merge their mom-and-pop operation with ours. She was a wonderful woman who wasn't quite ready to part with their "baby." Since they were doing okay with the sales of the product, she had to be convinced to let it grow into something much bigger. Unless I could get her on board, the transaction would never take place.

I firmly believe that it's better to be a presence with a name and a face than it is to be a ghost. I want to be the nice guy who is buying the family business, not the unknown businessman who is trying to take away everything they've worked so hard to achieve. Even when the principal shares the details of the transaction with his spouse, he often doesn't share the bigger-picture plan, which is something I like to do before moving forward.

If the transaction does move forward, you are, in essence, getting married. Consider the initial get-together akin to meeting your potential in-laws. Naturally, you should treat them with the same kind of respect you'd show to your intended's family. I spend the first thirty or forty minutes being humble and talking niceties to ease everyone's nerves. Once I can tell the angst has subsided, I begin to talk business. I talk to them about their long-term goals and what their future might look like if we move forward together. In addition to answering whatever questions they may have, I often lead them on a tour of our facility, introduce them to other key staff, and give them a sense that they'd genuinely be welcomed into our family. However, I also look for signs of incompatibility. On a few occasions, I have met with the spouses and decided not to do the transaction because the fit simply wasn't there.

Presenting yourself this way isn't hard to do, but it takes a lot of patience, perseverance, and tenacity. Endearing yourself to the spouse and then having the patience as he or she takes in the opportunity and thinks about the bigger picture always works in your favor. Many times the spouse ends up selling the principal, helping make the transaction happen. And that's exactly what occurred with the wife of the software principal. Once she could see the bigger picture, she got on board. Since then, I've sold a portion of that company, and everyone involved reaped the rewards, including the reluctant wife and her husband.

ORTHODOX PATH: Never meet the family.

SPARKS PATH: Meet the spouse early and confirm complete buy-in of the overall vision. Persuade the spouse that your goal is to succeed and provide for his or her family as you provide for your own family.

The Takeaway

Mastering the takeaway is one of the most important skills you can have when negotiating a transaction. Because negotiations are like a giant, high-stakes poker game: if the cards are turning sour, you have to be willing to walk away from the table before you lose everything. Taking your offer off the table is the ultimate smack down. If you play that card, even as a bluff, you must be willing to follow through until the bitter end. There's potential for things to come to a crashing halt, an outcome you need to be prepared to accept. But most of the time, the takeaway tactic gets the seller or whomever you're negotiating your transaction with to come to the table once and for all.

Everyone wants what he or she can't have. It's like taking a toy away from a child. The second you take away the toy, the child wants it more than ever. Likewise, when you take your offer off the table, the seller usually becomes more motivated to close the transaction. He or she can't stand the idea of not having something that's desired. Taking the offer off the table creates a sense of urgency and failure, two emotional responses that usually net a positive result: after that point, the transactions tend to close, and close fast.

Find a Second Interested Party

Going through a negotiation is somewhat similar to a courtship. When two guys are interested in the prettiest girl at the dance, a lot of magic starts to happen—and that's exactly the feeling you want to create when selling a business. You have to dance if you want to tango. In business, having another interested party makes the value of your company skyrocket. It creates a "last call" feeling that generates tremendous fervor, stirs excitement, and instills an urgency to close the deal. Even if you have a second party who's not really interested and you know it, you certainly can use their inquiries to your advantage by dropping hints to the other company without revealing the truth. When a company owner believes he or she is going to lose a transaction to someone else, especially a competitor, the owner will move mountains to get a deal done, even if it means improving the terms of the transaction. Often, he or she will give up a lot to make it happen.

Much like the takeaway—if you play this card, you have to be willing to see it through. If you dangle another company as a negotiating tool, understand there is a chance that the buyer will walk. Still, I am a big believer that, in general, people want what they can't have, so for me, it's usually worth the risk.

Summarize Transaction Agreements Immediately and in Writing

Once the other party and I come to a mutual understanding of the general terms of any transaction, I immediately write them on a single sheet of paper. This is a recap of everything we discussed and agreed to. I send this summary to the other principal involved within hours of the conversation. I keep the note simple and to the point by bulleting each of the items we agreed to do. This isn't a legal document drafted by an attorney; it's meant to be a nonbinding term sheet between the principal and me. I do this so no one strays from the agreed-upon terms, so we're clear about what we both heard, and so we're all kept on the same page.

Doing this small exercise has saved every transaction in which I have been involved over the years. It eliminates confusion, speculation, and interpretation. It's dangerous to assume that each party has heard the same thing. Without fail, adjustments are made to the terms if they aren't recorded. Not having this degree of clarity up front could jeopardize the transaction and result in a significant waste of time, energy, and resources on both sides. A term sheet with bulleted items confirms what everyone heard in that initial meeting and keeps the wheels on the bus moving forward.

ORTHODOX PATH: Start preparing legal documents for a transaction.

SPARKS PATH: Prepare a simple email summarizing the highlights of the terms as you understand them. This process will drastically smooth out the wrinkles and help avoid misunderstandings later.

Be Willing to Fail Fast

Many successful companies are willing to lose or fail sometimes . . . because that means they are out there trying new ideas, concepts, products, and delivery methods. Google has experienced far more failures than successes. Google Health, Google+, Google Answers, and Google PowerMeter are just four examples of start-up attempts that languished, and several more acquisition failures could easily be added to the list. Yet Google thrives as the world's leading search engine—one of the most profitable web-based businesses on the planet. Google is well known for empowering its team members to explore their own projects for a set amount of time each week, which has led to great things. Google's willingness to allow staff members to think outside the box means the people in charge believe in the power of failure. Without it, there would be no success.

I keep articles on failure in my briefcase, and every now and then I read them to remind myself that failure leads to growth, greater knowledge, and experience. Did you know that the first Ford motorcar didn't have a reverse gear? Can you imagine how dumbfounded the earliest customers felt when they pulled in front of their horse barns and called out to their family and friends to come and see what they'd just bought . . . only to discover that they couldn't back the car up?

Just so you know you're in good company, the average entrepreneur fails 3.8 times before succeeding. This proves that you learn as much from losing as you gain from winning.

We live in a society in which mistakes are often frowned

upon, especially in the workplace. While I have no patience for incompetence or laziness, I have a strong appreciation for the benefits of taking a wrong turn along the way. Have you ever been on a road trip where you've veered off the beaten path? Most of the time, you find yourself making discoveries about places, people, and sites you never would have seen if you hadn't changed your course. These are usually the best experiences, because they are the most unexpected.

Think about the Wright Brothers, Albert Einstein, and even Steve Jobs—all pioneers and leaders who took a few hits along the way to get to the mountaintop each was steadily climbing. When was the last time you tried something new? Perhaps you tried to learn a new language, take up a new sport, or start your own company. Did you make any mistakes along the way? We all have, and it is our mistakes that teach us the most about everything we are trying to learn . . . and they are especially valuable in business. I assure you that the road from insight to discovery is not straight. There will be bumps along the way, but it is important to remember that a bend in the road is not the end of the road. Most great achievements have come from meandering paths of misjudgment and false turns. The trick is to be strategic about the errors we allow and the lessons we take with us as we continue to grow and move forward.

The point is, you will fail along the journey to success—guaranteed! It's how you deal with failure that determines how well you succeed. Own that thought and embrace it when it happens because failure is a good thing. The key to overcoming failure is not to wallow in it for more time than you need—for me that is somewhere around thirty minutes—because any longer than that just wastes precious time. You paid for that failure, so you may as well take that knowledge and do something much greater with it than feeling sorry for yourself.

I have never partnered with an entrepreneur who hasn't failed before we met. Someone who has failed brings better experience to the table than someone who is so green that he or she has never failed. The entrepreneur who has failed possesses two necessary qualities—willingness to take risks and courage to live with the consequences of those results. Failure is a great part of the journey. If you don't embrace that notion, you are fooling yourself.

"Nothing in this world can take the place of persistence. Talent will not; nothing is more common than unsuccessful men with talent. Genius will not; unrewarded genius is almost a proverb. Education will not; the world is full of educated derelicts. Persistence and determination alone are omnipotent. The slogan 'Press On!' has solved and always will solve the problems of the human race." —Calvin Coolidge

Learn to Live Debt-Free

Most of us have grown up with decades of exposure to the you'll-always-have-a-payment mentality. We've been conditioned to believe that car payments, mortgages, student loans, and credit cards are not only acceptable, they are actually normal. They've been touted as symbols of responsibility and status. Juggling the stress of these obligations has been elevated to an art form—one that is burying most people in debt from which they'll never recover.

A lot of people think that just because the bank *gave* them a loan (note the emphasis on the word "gave") and they *got* a car, the bank is like Santa Claus handing out gifts. But you are the customer/client in this transaction; you're the one paying for everything. And while the customer is usually the one calling the shots, we all know that the banks abide by a different set of rules, including the one that says, "He who has the gold makes the rules." You'll see this rule in effect the minute you are late, miss a payment, or stop paying altogether on your loans. You'll instantly go from customer to deadbeat. Many consumers have it backward, thinking they are lucky to get financed when, in fact, doing so is often the worst financial decision of their lives.

When Darren Hardy and I first talked about possible topics for my book, one of the things he shared with me was the influence my philosophy on debt and living stress-free has had on his life. He encouraged me to share my beliefs on why it is better to live debt-free so others might have the opportunity to see their financial life through a different lens.

Living debt-free has helped me find tremendous clarity in all areas of my life. I am mentally secure and far better off because I never worry about paying off debt. It is a tremendous load off my shoulders to know I can walk out my front door every morning without any concern about how I am going to make ends meet. Living debt-free clears my mind of all of that tension. And really, who wants or needs more worries in their lives?

I maintain an authentic and commonsense approach to people, life, and business. I've rarely carried any debt, because owing someone else money always gives me a level of anxiety that is uncomfortable and awkward. For as long as I can recall, my car, home, and credit card balances have been at zero.

When a bill comes in, I pay it—early. I do this for everything, from vendor invoices to my taxes. I've never understood the "robbing Peter to pay Paul" approach to finances. If you can't pay for something when you buy it, you can't afford it. It's really that simple.

I have always believed that carrying a mortgage is an awful financial decision. Oh, you'll find plenty of financial advisers who are dead-set against paying cash for a home. These experts argue that you would receive a better rate of return by investing your money elsewhere. And generally, dollar for dollar, they are correct. For most people, the purchase of a home is the single largest purchase they will ever make. An all-cash purchase should be viewed as a no-mortgage investment. The return is the rate you would otherwise have paid on the mortgage but have now successfully avoided.

For many cash buyers, a sense of security and confidence is more important and healthier than their rate of return. In addition, cash buyers have 100 percent equity walking out of closing, and that equity is accessible for emergencies. And, cash buyers don't pay any interest on borrowed money. Even with the low interest rates being offered these days, those amounts quickly add up. Unless the benefits of the tax deduction outweigh the benefits of stability and security, pay cash!

Look, I've had $80,000 homes and multimillion-dollar homes over the course of my life, and I paid them all off. I understand that most people can't pay cash for their homes from the start. In that case, I always encourage people to pay that mortgage down as quickly as possible. One of my longest-standing handwritten goals is to maintain a debt-free life and always pay off my cars and homes as soon as I can.

I cannot overstate the point that living mortgage-free provides access to quick cash in a financial emergency. You never know when there is going to be a rainy day need, but you will be awfully glad you are prepared when it starts to pour! When I lost Unistar, as I mentioned earlier in this book, I was able to use the 100 percent equity I had in my home to help me get through the sudden and unexpected loss. Going back to work in the insurance industry wasn't a possibility, so my choices were pretty limited. Thankfully, I had something major to fall back on. This certainty gave me the desperately needed start-up seed capital to launch my new business venture. If I hadn't had the available equity in my home to pull from, I might not have been able to restart my obliterated career.

There are other benefits to paying cash for your home, especially in today's sluggish real estate market. In a softening real estate market, sellers may be more inclined to lower the price of the home for buyers who don't have to jump through lenders' hoops to meet eligibility requirements to secure a loan. These days, fewer people are able to get approved for loans, so being able to pay with cash, or even paying a major portion in cash, provides the leverage you need to negotiate a lower price on the home and a better interest rate with the bank. Paying in cash also cuts down considerably on the amount of administrative fees and paperwork involved at the close.

My debt-free philosophy holds true for cars, too. A car is an expensive proposition to begin with; you have to pay for insurance, gas, repairs, and maintenance. A car payment magnifies all of this. In fact, if you total the expenses you pay each year to own a car, you'll see why your money seems to disappear into thin air. For most people, a car is the second most expensive budget item after a home.

Paying cash for everything means you can afford it. Simply stated, most people use credit to fulfill a temporary desire for something they don't really need. Credit card companies are very good at luring people into debt—sending out cards, giving them to college students and young people in their first jobs, and gradually increasing the credit limits until they are higher than an entire month's income, so you can't possibly ever pay them off in full. Credit cards can be as addictive as a drug, but in the case of credit cards, the pusher comes to you in the form of an envelope delivered right to your front door! According to bankruptcy lawyers, if your credit card debt is equal to your annual salary, you will never be able to get out of debt. You are, in essence, bankrupt. If you are in that situation, it's time to get super-honest with yourself—and fast.

Being free of debt enables you to use money for the extra things in life that you want, conscience-free. It enables you to enjoy life more fully because you can spend your hard-earned money on the things that you want instead of need. This includes going on family vacations or paying for your kid's college tuition without worry.

Living without debt also enables you to save for the future. Because they were unable to save enough money for the future earlier in their careers, many people are still working during the period of their lives when they ought to be enjoying retirement. When money has to go toward bills, it can't go into savings or investments. Instead of living comfortably as a senior citizen, they are forced to go back to work. And in the state of high unemployment we are all facing, that's especially challenging for older people. Being out of debt gives you the chance to give your family a better life. If you've got kids, you can pay for their sports teams, music lessons, karate classes, or other activities. In turn, this allows them to use their gifts to build their strengths, and generally grow into more well-rounded individuals. Being out of debt also ensures that when your kids have kids someday, you'll have enough money put away to enjoy your golden years—and spoil your grandkids!

It may take months or years of living carefully and doing without, but the sense of accomplishment and true peace you gain when you are no longer a slave to your debt is your reward. Peace of mind is worth the discomfort of financial discipline—and before long, you will have adjusted to your new lifestyle.

Financial freedom is just a decision away. Just do it!

Learn from My Failures

While writing this book, I found it challenging to go back into the business archives in my head. I have a unique ability to be done with a subject when it is over and gone. I erase the files of failure in my mind so I can go back and record over them. I think of it as clearing up more space on my hard drive. I don't waste time on the past because I am all about the present and the future.

Look, what happened yesterday is history—it's in the past, and that is where I like to leave it. The only way to live in the moment is to be in the moment. In the here and now. If I lose money and time on an investment, I don't crawl into the fetal position and cry about it. I lick my wounds and reflect on what I learned. Then I move on! I have said it before in many different ways, but it worth repeating: you will have challenges and failures—recovering quickly is key to achieving outrageous success.

One of the best examples of this resilience is when I decided to start Traders Television Network (TTV). There was a gentleman from Dallas who had successfully built several television networks and an incredible facility using satellites. He eventually sold his company in the 1990s for over $400 million. At the time, satellite television was in its infancy, so airtime was relatively cheap. The blush was coming off that rose, but I thought his business model was intriguing enough to look at for possible ways we could pick up where he left off. I was specifically interested in creating a private network for retail stock and options traders. This was also the time when online stock trading was really taking off.

Just as we first started kicking the tires on TTV, a salesman from a major satellite television network came into our office offering cheap airtime through their satellite distribution system. Admittedly, my curiosity was piqued, but first I needed to understand how it worked. The salesman systematically went through the mechanics, including the need for customers to install a separate dedicated satellite dish on their homes to receive the programming. At first glance, it was a logistical nightmare. And then I asked about cost.

"How cheap is cheap?" I was curious.

"There's a $150,000 monthly operating fee. That's the cost you'd have to pay for us to provide your programming distribution."

Well, that was a nonstarter! "I've got another meeting to go to," I said, as I politely got up and walked out of the room.

Until they could simplify the equipment needs by installing a single dish on a customer's roof, significantly reducing the cost of distribution for us, I had absolutely no interest. That is until two years later—after I sold GlobalTec Solutions and started building a cutting-edge, state-of-the-art, live television studio at Splash Media.

Even though I knew the concept was challenged, I never stopped thinking about the possibility of providing content to our online stock-trading customers through television. Remember, this was 2004, a year before YouTube was even launched. At the time, there were no other means to access this type of content; training videos or "edu-tainment" shows on the Internet didn't exist the way they do today. If you did streaming video through the World Wide Web, most people were still on dial-up, so it was slow and painful to watch while the footage buffered every few seconds. Television appeared to be the logical choice for us.

Even though I had just sold GlobalTec Solutions to a company in Florida, I knew there were thousands of active GlobalTec software users and evangelists who were eager to be educated. There had to be a way to provide them with a live-market GlobalTec education product for a reasonable monthly fee (the all-important recurring revenue factor we always look for!). After all, we were very successful at doing this via streaming audio on the Internet before I sold the company. I was certain these customers had an appetite for stock-trading information and stock-trading software products and were willing to spend money to satisfy that need. I was sure that a recurring fee model would be magical if I could figure out a way to provide the programming. The biggest challenge was whether we could build a product—a television show that was live during the markets' hours and could be broadcast into people's homes.

For this idea to work, we would have to partner up with the company to which I had just sold GlobalTec Solutions, while we were still in the honeymoon phase of the sale. Internally, everyone was excited about the possibilities of launching our own network, but we didn't go to the new owners of GlobalTec right away. I wanted to work through the concept, build the box, develop the product (which already existed as audio online training education, or what we referred to as "edu-tainment"), and then brand it all. The goal was to educate, via entertainment, about trading.

Naturally, the first thing I did was ask my graphic designer Megan to come up with a logo for TTV so it would look like an independent, third-party network. We were using the GlobalTec Solution's software tools and some of the same personalities we had used in previous productions to help us figure out how the show could work. It took about five months to get it all figured out before we presented it to the new owner of GlobalTec Solutions. After I was satisfied that all systems were a go, I decided that my partner in this venture, Chris Kraft, and I would pitch the idea at the company Christmas party.

The new owner of GlobalTec Solutions had come to Dallas from Florida for the party. The representatives from the satellite provider were also there to sign our agreement. It had taken three months of negotiations, but we had finally struck a deal with a major satellite provider, and we were set to sign the deal the night of the party. Chris Kraft was in a room upstairs waiting for the hotel concierge to bring up the signed agreement with the satellite provider, while I was in another room getting ready to make our presentation to the new owners of GlobalTec Solutions.

Keep in mind that we had already started recruiting talent and hiring people to work at TTV. In the event they didn't bite, Plan B was to go to a GlobalTec Solutions competitor and pitch the programming idea to them, though I really hoped to avoid doing that. I knew the GlobalTec customer very well, and it was a perfect match. We were building "the box" and the network name while developing eleven hours of live shows a day to be shot and broadcast from the studio ... all without the new owners of GlobalTec signing on to the idea yet. They knew we were working on something, but they had no idea of the scope. Luckily, the new owner of GlobalTec Solutions and I had become friends. We were in the trenches together for years before he bought the company from me. I didn't think there would be a lot of resistance or push back from him because I knew he would see the bigger opportunity in TTV. If he agreed, we would be the first to market, which gave this venture every element I look for when getting involved with a product.

Of course the new owner signed on to the idea, so all systems were a go. We went on an eighteen-city tour with our personalities (faces of the product) and behind-the-scenes team, promoting our product to our evangelistic GlobalTec customers. They loved the idea; however, shortly after our launch, I heard those fateful words, "Houston, we have a problem!"

The greatest benefit of moving through life at Sparks Speed is being able to identify successes fast and failures even faster. Three months after we launched TTV, we realized it wasn't going to work due to our distribution method. The programming and content were off-the-charts great! People who could see it loved it! However, the cost to the consumer was still too high. If you already had television cable or another satellite dish installed at your home, we had to convince you to sign yet another contract with our satellite provider to receive TTV. That essentially turned us into a satellite retailer for our provider. If by chance, you had a satellite dish from the company we were affiliated with, you still needed to have a different satellite dish installed to receive our programming.

Our mistake was that we trusted the provider to deliver what they promised. Unfortunately, our idea was ahead of the curve. By the time I could see clearly where we were heading, I had already sunk close to $7 million into this venture. It was time to take the spanking and move on. That one left a scar!

Working with Millennials

I am a classic baby boomer. I grew up with a firm understanding that hard work, tenacity, and perseverance eventually pay off. When I was starting out in business, people came out of college with a willingness to begin at the bottom and work their way up the corporate ladder. They were ready to take on even the most menial tasks because they understood what was expected if they wanted to get ahead. There was an inherent respect for their superiors, and everyone was filled with desire to learn from their experiences. It was a "yes sir, no sir" society. I never once complained about sweeping floors or performing tedious tasks that might have been beneath someone else in my position. To this day, I have no issues taking out the trash, sweeping the sidewalk outside our doors, passing out the mail, or doing anything else in the name of building a successful image and business.

Fast-forward to the year 2014. That do-what-it-takes mentality is as obsolete as a good Bernie Madoff investment. It's a whole new generation, one I've affectionately dubbed *Generation WTF,* commonly referred to as millennials. (Disclaimer: obviously not everyone in this generation falls into this category, but sadly, the supermajority in this demographic does.) Equally as amazing, now you can find tons of books, lectures, CDs, and professional consultants (e.g., www.travisrobertson.com) ready to help you navigate this bizarre culture in our largest workforce.

For would-be entrepreneurs who will be hiring, just know that millennials are clearly and profoundly cut from a different cloth. I recently read that millennials are also the most cynical and distrusting generation ever recorded. Only 19 percent think most people can be trusted. According to a study from the Pew Research Center, millennials are less attached to marriage, religion, and political institutions than Generation Xers, baby boomers, and the other demographic flavors journalists love to use. According to the study, they like their friends, their digital social networks, and their toys . . . and that's about it. I am utterly amazed by how many people between the ages of twenty-one and thirty-five walk through our doors with a "What have you done for me lately?" attitude—even before they've been hired! The sense of entitlement from this generation is astounding and renders me speechless. A recent California State University study showed that, when asked, *81 percent* of the students believed they should be entitled to free college tuition, free healthcare, the guarantee of a job, a government-provided down payment to buy a house, government guarantee for retirement, and money for themselves after taxing the rich. These views are obviously a bit communistic, like North Korea, China, and Russia . . . and you have seen how that turned out.

These days, you're lucky if you get a millennial to show up regularly. They throw a backpack over their shoulder, slip in a pair of earbuds, turn the music up on their iPhone, and all but flip you off as they walk in or out the door. I genuinely worry about where our country will be in the next thirty years with this generation's lack of give-a-damn. I believe that the "everyone gets a trophy" syndrome is starting to come to roost. The point is that everyone should not be first place winner every single time he or she takes on a challenge. If everyone is always winning, then we have nothing to strive for. Losing a few times is what makes winning so much sweeter. Second place is the first loser, and getting defeated builds character. I don't fail; I learn ways something won't work. I deny failure!

Splash Media's outsourced social media services were so successful that we oversold our ability to train, staff up, and fulfill. Compound this with the fact that we were trying to figure out how to deal with the millennial workforce attitude, and we were sitting on a time bomb waiting to explode. We had over a hundred trained social media millennials in an office of about 120 people. We had 150 percent turnover of staff our first year. Millennials were being hired a half dozen per week and quitting six months later, ten at a time. It was a revolving door! Our clients were not amused, either. Out of the thousands of people I have hired and dozens of businesses I have started, I have never witnessed such disrespect for a job.

Would-be entrepreneurs, you are fully warned. Ask anyone with a child between the ages of twenty and thirty, and most will tell you that their kids are working in some form of social media within their jobs. These kids don't worry about their jobs because they have no fear, which is not always a bad thing if bridled with a dose of reality. They think they can go out and do the same thing with someone else and continue to survive. You see, the difference for them is that they are happy to merely survive and flop on the sofa at a friend's apartment. I'm not content to survive. I always seek ways to thrive. The good Lord gave us tremendous assets like a brain, eyes, ears, a nose, mouth, arms, legs, and emotions—what a waste it is to merely survive! Worms and crickets merely survive—human beings are on this earth to thrive.

Generation WTF also thinks that job-hopping is cool—that it gives them leverage. But to a business owner, it's a setup for disaster. I am not interested in hiring someone who has worked ten or fifteen jobs in a five-year period. Those folks are a lousy bet because you know they have no staying power. Without hesitation, I put those résumés straight into the trash bin.

I had a young lady come into my office for an interview; she was incredibly proud of the fact that she had worked eight different six-month jobs in the course of just four years. Instead of hiring her, I used the opportunity to warn her that she was likely to be one job away from never working again. She was totally shocked by my statement. I think she expected me to be equally impressed with her résumé. I explained that she lacked commitment, longevity, and loyalty—three things I look for when making the decision to hire and train someone.

"No one will want to invest in you. It takes time to get you up to speed on what we do, what we want you to do, and how our company and products work," I told her. "That costs a lot of money. You are a liability for a considerable amount of time to a company—not an asset."

And the reality is, it can take six months or longer to get someone to cross over from costing money to making it for your company. The last thing I want to do is hire someone and have her working at my company for six months while plotting her next move to a competitor.

There's tremendous importance in pulling your weight. I don't expect new team members to sit in on high-level marketing meetings and own the company in six months, but I do expect them to want to be in that position in two years' time. If you don't want that, you are hurting yourself because you are not using that window to learn. You are not maturing or refining your ability to effectively communicate. People will not hire you because they will not trust you. I won't put money into people who are going to bolt the first chance they get.

The staff turnover in social media companies is extremely high. A simple LinkedIn ad for a social media manager might result in a thousand or more résumés in less than twenty-four hours. Of those candidates, maybe thirty are somewhat qualified, and perhaps ten of those will even show up for an interview. And if one does get the job and is asked to join our team, he or she often comes in with an incredibly cocky attitude.

Granted, social media is more prone to these personality types, but almost every entrepreneur today will tell you a similar story about the young up-and-comers in their company. For every one of these millennials, there are a hundred more waiting around the corner to take his or her place—none of whom are really as interested in doing the work as in getting the paycheck.

It's frustrating for business owners to staff up because, while society is screaming about the lack of available jobs out there, the majority of this generation doesn't want to work in what they perceive as "just any old job." They want the keys to the executive washroom, a company car, and a six-figure salary without ever putting in a single day's worth of hard work. They have a dangerous combination of ignorance and arrogance that will eventually lead to their fall . . . or worse, our country's fall.

My advice to those considering employing the vast millennial generation: Do your research first. Go to seminars and hire a consultant to help you navigate the phenomena.

My advice to the millennial generation is simple. **DO THE TIME, OBSERVE, LISTEN!** Class has really just begun. You will gain so much more where you are than where you are going. Commit at least two years to each job you take, and become an expert. When you decide to move up the ladder, always give a thirty-day notice to vacate, not the customary two weeks. Thirty days is so much more respectful to your employer, and instead of resenting you, the employer you're leaving will applaud you and wish you well on your journey.

Even if you don't know it, the experience you are getting is worth much more than your paycheck. Not long ago, we had an extraordinarily bright young lady working at Splash Media. I could have envisioned her managing one of our divisions in the near future. She was an absolute triple-threat rock star. She was one of the youngest on our team, but I saw clearly that she had the ability to be the best we had. She was worth the effort . . . and then out of the blue, she took a position at a major cosmetics firm and left us with no notice. A few months later, I noticed on LinkedIn that she left that firm for another job in another state.

No matter where you choose to work, be willing to stick with it. Be willing to sweep the floors if you have to so you can learn your business from the ground up. Even if you are working at a fast-food restaurant, bear in mind that you might someday become a franchise owner; the little things you learn along the way will be valuable things to know. That's the true path to achievement and success in a time where nothing is guaranteed.

ORTHODOX PATH: Job-hop your way up the ladder.

SPARKS PATH: Do the work! Watch, listen, and learn. Class starts when you get the job. Soon enough you will be at the top of the ladder looking down.

More Davids Than Goliaths

Entrepreneurs really are a different breed. Most of us have a clear vision of where we are going and what we want to achieve at the end of the day. We get off track when we start listening to too many naysayers or people with traditional opinions of how everything "should be."

It's absolute BS!

If you want to stay true to your vision and dream, go ahead and listen to other people's opinions, but take them with a grain of salt. Remember, no one but you has to walk in your shoes. If you're clear about the end game and clear in your vision, you will always walk the right path to lead you there.

Two thousand years ago, there were two warring Israeli tribes. One day the kings of these tribes said they had had enough of killing each other's citizens and wanted to settle this battle once and for all. They decided that each king could pick one man from his tribe to fight the other to the death.

One king picked Goliath, a virtual killing machine who was nearly eight feet tall and who weighed over 400 pounds. Goliath could take down a dozen men at once. The other king asked his citizens for a volunteer who was willing to fight Goliath to the end. Only one man stepped forward—David. David was just short of six feet tall and was very thin and wiry. Upon seeing this far-less-physical match for Goliath, the king continued to ask for others to step forward. Despite his pleas, nobody else would consider certain death against Goliath.

When they realized it would be a battle of David versus Goliath, the citizens said, "We might as well concede, as there is no way David can win."

Desperate, the king responded, "We must try or we will lose our freedom!"

The battle date was set, and David was summoned to begin training with his king's best soldiers. The first thing the soldiers gave David was a huge, heavy sword. David started to swing it around, but he could hardly raise it over his shoulder. Next, the soldiers put a suit of armor on David. The armor was so substantial that he could not bend over or walk, let alone fight. Things weren't looking very good. Finally, the soldiers placed leather boots on David so he could withstand the heat of the sand under his feet while fighting. David could hardly walk in the boots; he was used to being nearly barefoot in his open sandals.

Dressed in full regalia—wearing the heavy armor and leather boots, and wielding the tree-trunk-like sword—David tried to mock-fight one of his trainers but failed miserably.

Undeterred, David said, "Enough! If I am going to die, I want to do it on my own terms and with my own plan!" He removed the armor, put his sandals back on his feet, and gathered his simple but very effective slingshot, a weapon in which he had total confidence.

You know the rest of the story. David knocked down Goliath with one stone, a shot delivered from that trusted slingshot. If David had listened to everyone around him, he never would have slain Goliath with a single stone. Instead, he believed in himself and his plan, which led him to a great victory.

In business, you will be faced with many Goliath-sized obstacles that appear insurmountable and impossible to conquer. In those moments, you must stay true to your ideas and your vision in order to succeed. As David did, you will demonstrate overwhelming tenacity and passion, you will stay your own course versus someone else's, and in the end you will slay the giant—whatever that giant represents for you. Showing the courage and willingness to stay the course also makes you a tremendously effective leader. Fear is nothing more than False Evidence Appearing Real. Don't give in to fear or other people's negative opinions. Stand firm and fight for what you believe. This is the true spirit of a great entrepreneur.

ORTHODOX PATH: Listen to all the opinions out there, and quit at the first sign of resistance.

SPARKS PATH: Listen to opinions with a grain of salt. Face the insurmountable odds, and conquer your Goliath!

It Sincerely Is a Journey

I have started, acquired, managed, and sold many companies over the course of my career . . . so many that I know a transaction isn't a done transaction until the money is in the bank. And when you finally do close a transaction, there's little in life that feels more satisfying. Twenty-five years ago, after months of negotiations, my team and I landed a major, A+ rated reinsurer to back the vast volume of insurance business we were writing. It was a very big win, perhaps life-changing. When all was said and done, I knew it would make my company a huge success. When our final meeting finished, I was certain we had come to reliable terms. I got into the front seat of our waiting town car, along with three other guys who were with me, and headed straight to the airport. All of us were silent, just grinning from ear to ear. That's when I turned, looked at them, and said, "Enjoy this moment, guys—take it all in because you are not going to get much happier than this. This is as good as it gets."

We had worked tirelessly to get this reinsurance treaty completed, and, while the success was not an immediate cash success, it *was* a major success in the world we were living in. Success comes in several forms, and that day, the form was tremendous gratification! At first, none of the guys understood why I said what I did. What I was trying to convey is that there is no better feeling in business than snagging that big fish, closing that transaction, and reaching that peak you have set out to climb. It is indeed a journey to get there, but it's so very worth it.

Years later, I exchanged emails with all of the guys who had been in the car that day, and every one of them acknowledged that he now understood what I meant. In that moment, they didn't realize that they had arrived at the place they worked so hard to reach. People are always *aiming* in their careers, and they often forget to just enjoy the roads they travel along the way. The journey truly is as important as the destination. There will always be big projects that work out just as you had hoped . . . and perhaps more that don't. But when it all comes together and everyone has left every single thing he or she had on the playing field, there's a feeling of pride and success that is hard to match.

You can always engage in more transactions, but you will never be happier than you are in that moment of closing a transaction. Take time to enjoy the journey because life passes us by pretty darn fast. If you don't stop and recognize the achievements you've attained, what's the point in pursuing them?

The great NFL coach Vince Lombardi once said, "I firmly believe that any man's finest hour—his greatest fulfillment to all he holds dear—is that moment when he has worked his heart out in a good cause and lies exhausted on the field of battle—victorious!"

ORTHODOX PATH: Success is defined by money.

SPARKS PATH: Success is defined by the journey you took and in achieving the goals you set out to achieve.

Questions and Answers with Marc Sparks

Many people have described me as mysterious—someone who keeps my thoughts and feelings close to the chest. In fact, when I first began writing this book, several of the people I spoke with about it along the way asked if it would provide a peek behind the curtain so they might finally get some insight into my personal story. I thought writing this book would answer a lot of their questions and I hope it does. In the interim, though, I came across a quiz in *INC.* magazine that posed the following questions to a dozen other business owners. Their answers intrigued me enough to fill in the blanks for myself. I thought it might be fun to share my answers with you here, as they shed light on the way I think and approach business. For added enjoyment, I added a few more questions to this Q&A. I hope you will take a few minutes to answer the questions for yourself as well.

1. When did you start your first business and what was it?

The first company I started was a manufacturing business I started in 1977. I was making two-inch thick, clear acrylic desk/trophy novelty pieces that were cut in the shape of Texas, on which I engraved a company or personal names and logos. I designed, manufactured, and sold thousands of these items from a one-third page color ad in *Texas Monthly* magazine.

2. What is the weirdest thing in your office?

A life-size ceramic pig. This piece reminds me that "pigs get fat, hogs get slaughtered," and to leave some meat on the bone for the next person to make sure he or she is getting a good trade.

3. Who do you wish would friend you on Facebook?

Jesus Christ, Jack Welch, Steve Jobs, Elon Musk, Warren Buffett, Henry Ford, Walt Disney, Bill Gates, Mother Teresa, and every president of the United States.

4. What business ideas do you wish you had come up with?

Search engines, auto insurance, paper clips, yellow sticky pads, and vitamin water.

5. Name five things about you that would surprise your staff and entrepreneur partners?

1) I can field-dress (gut) a deer in less than six minutes.

2) I struggle daily to feel emotionally and financially "full."

3) I have remarkable reflexes. My reflexes are like a superhero's reflexes might be. If someone's cup is falling off a table, I have the ability to reach under it and save it from crashing to the floor. It happens automatically! Hundreds of times in my life people have witnessed my quick reflexes in action and have said, "Okay, that was cool . . . but really weird."

4) I was once six feet two. (Not really. I'm five feet six and a half.) I didn't know I was vertically challenged until my wife of nearly thirty years mentioned it at a party a few years ago. Overconfidence has its benefits!

5) I traveled completely around the earth in twenty-six days.

6. What is one thing from your early days that you are still holding onto?

My 1967 All-Star Little League baseball pendant.

7. What kind of student were you in high school?

Out of six classes, I would have one A (if the teacher liked me), two Bs, and three Cs.

8. What kind of kid were you in high school?

Athletic . . . and the class clown.

9. What's the most fun you have had at work?

The day I rang the opening bell on Wall Street for my company, Unistar. (I cried a little . . .)

10. If you could do anything in the world today, what would you do?

I would run/moderate a "think tank" whereby if I called you, you had to show up.

11. If you were dictator for a day, what would you do first?

I would abolish the IRS, along with current federal and state income taxes, and charge a flat tax of 15 percent on all retail sales at all times. The states would keep 5 percent, Uncle Sam would get 10 percent, and everyone would have to live within that budget. I would also outlaw lobbyists on a state and federal level.

12. In your opinion, what are the common traits of successful people?

- Successful people are habitual people, and they form daily routines.

- They are extremely confident!

- They are always learning.

- They always perform and do exactly what they say they will do.

- They are passionate about their product or service.

- They have eliminated the word "can't" from their vocabulary.

- They are hardworking, and always looking for what else they can do.

- The majority of them are healthy—they eat well and exercise.

13. What kind of products do you like to invest your time and money in (not in order of importance)?

- Products that have an element of recurring monthly revenue in them.

- Products that are ultra-easy to understand (by a third grader).

- Products that have a super-simple message for marketing purposes.

- Products that have a passionate, tenacious entrepreneur behind them.

14. What do you regret the most as a serial entrepreneur?

- Not firing disruptive people faster.

- Not pruning the "noise" out of my life faster.

15. If there was only one thing for an entrepreneur to remember 18 months after reading this book, what would it be?

The Unorthodox Path to Outrageous Success is to focus on developing your packaging (website, brochures, slicks, and box) first, and then the rest will come. It's counterintuitive to develop marketing materials first, but you'll dig up tons of gold for your product during the journey.

16. What are the top twenty-five (okay, twenty-six) takeaways that you want to leave someone who has read this book?

1) Produce the packaging first, and the rest will follow.

2) Deny failure's grip! Failure is simply a lesson in what not to do next time.

3) If a third grader can't understand it, make it so one can or don't do it!

4) Find your passion to invest in; it's not work if you do.

5) Be willing to sacrifice; cut the BS and do what it takes to get it done.

6) Hustle like your life depends on winning.

7) Be ready to zig when you are zagging, as challenges will come at you hard and fast.

8) Hire people smarter than you. Much smarter!

9) Fire talented but disruptive people quickly.

10) Give back.

11) Find a spiritual being that you believe in (have faith).

12) Pick a role model, and emulate that person.

13) Listen a lot more than you talk.

14) Be the first to market at all costs.

15) Make key staff shareholders/owners.

16) Laugh a lot.

17) Be habitual; form daily routines and habits that make you feel really good.

18) Always have a daily dashboard for your business. Don't wait. Do it today.

19) Always do what you say you will do, even if you lose money doing so.

20) Prune! Look for noise you can prune out of your life each day.

21) Exercise a minimum of three times a week, for your mind as much as for your body.

22) Read every book and listen to every audio session that Darren Hardy has ever produced.

23) When you think you are done for the day, just do one more thing.

24) Run from people who suck the life out of you.

25) Assess your top six friends once a year. Are you better or worse by association?

26) If you are not early to every commitment, you are late.

Suggested Resources

The Compound Effect by Darren Hardy (actually, all of his books and audios)

Challenge to Succeed: A Philosophy for Successful Living by Jim Rohn

Think and Grow Rich by Napoleon Hill

The Happiness Advantage: The Seven Principles of Positive Psychology That Fuel Success and Performance at Work by Shawn Achor

Crush It! Why Now Is the Time to Cash in on Your Passion by Gary Vaynerchuk

Rework by Jason Fried and David Heinemeier Hanson

The Dressmaker of Khair Khana: Five Sisters, One Remarkable Family, and the Woman Who Risked Everything to Keep Them Safe by Gayle Tzemach Lemmon

Kiss Theory Good Bye: Five Proven Ways to Get Extraordinary Results in Any Company by Bob Prosen

KFC in China: Secret Recipe for Success by Warren K. Liu

Just Do It by Art Williams (speech), www.youtube.com/watch?v=b2uFH0NCMY4

About the Author

M arc Sparks is the entrepreneurs' entrepreneur! If you look in the dictionary under "serial entrepreneur," you will see Marc's picture. Since he graduated from high school in Austin, Texas, in 1975, Marc has been a principal in dozens of start-ups . . . some outrageously successful and some downright disasters; however, Marc says he learned volumes from the disastrous ventures. After thirty-four years of entrepreneurialism, Marc finally put his journey and kernels of wisdom on paper for others to learn from his experiences.

Marc's book, *They Can't Eat You*, was painful for him to write because he shares everything—warts and all! Sparks says, "I feel like anyone reading my book will learn much more from my unsuccessful ventures than they will learn from my successful ones. It's easy for me to say, 'Look at me—I started a software company and sold $200 million a year worth of our product,' but it's much more educational for me to say, 'Look at me—I started an insurance holding company out of my back bedroom and built it to nearly a billion dollar market cap and then lost it all in a ninety-day period of time.' My colleagues convinced me to write the book, and I figured if I were going to do it, I would want my experience to be a blessing for someone. My book is for those entrepreneurs who are losing 'hope' and just can't seem to get across the goal line with their dreams."

Sparks's business passion is clearly to build companies—often from ideas that others think cannot be done. Sparks maintains a handful of portfolio companies in his "private" private equity firm, Timber Creek Capital, LP (www.timbercreekcapital.com). Taking an initial idea, he proceeds to establish not only the business model but the company culture and to develop both the short-term goals and the long-range growth plans. Sparks manages by example, setting the patterns for his entire team to follow. "My door is always open; we meet in real time: right NOW! Everyone calls it 'Sparks Speed.' I figure by the time you set up a meeting and reserve conference rooms, you could just resolve the challenge instead."

Marc is often asked two questions: "Aren't you afraid of losing?" and "How do you do it?"

Marc answers: "To sum it up, call it ignorance or a gift, I have no fear of losing it all. It sounds a little weird; however, as long as I can pay my bills, have a roof over my head, and be with my family, I'm happy. Don't get me wrong; I love to win, but I just can't win them all! It's life! I have never said I want to be a millionaire. Being rich to me is having great health, a healthy family, good friends, building a successful business from scratch, and having hundreds of happy staff members and thousands of happy customers . . . that's a great day! I believe that God gave me a special 'shutoff valve' that somehow eliminates the fear factor. I have so little fear that sometimes I wonder if there is something wrong with me. My lack of fear of losing is probably due to my upbringing, and that the poorest I can remember being is when I had to buy groceries at a Texaco convenience store/gas station with my Texaco credit card. I remember to this day that while I was poor, I was still excited about life and passionate about my journey to come."

How does Marc do it? Faith, Passion, Tenacity, Focus, Savvy of Monetization, and—most important—an Outrageous Sense of Urgency (aka Sparks Speed). As an entrepreneur, you will rely on all these qualities often. Mix these honed-in qualities with treating people the way you want to be treated—fairly, with respect and honesty—and *you will succeed!*

Want to contact Marc Sparks personally?

- **Personal Websites:**
  www.MarcSparks.com
  www.WhoIsMarcSparks.com

- **Business Website:** www.TimberCreekCapital.com

- 🔗 www.linkedin.com/in/marcsparks

- 📘 www.facebook.com/marc.sparks1

- 🐦 www.twitter.com/msparks5010

Notes

Notes

Notes

Notes

Notes